D0152643

FEB -- 2012
37653002409574
Main NonFiction: 5th floor
823 SCOTT
Sir Walter Scott

Central Arkansas Library System
Little Rock Public Library
100 Rock Street
Little Rock, Arkansas 72201

2/95   GAYLORD MG

Sir Walter Scott
Revised Edition

By John Lauber
University of Alberta

Twayne Publishers
A Division of G. K. Hall & Co. • *Boston*

950438

Sir Walter Scott, Revised Edition
John Lauber

Copyright 1989 by G. K. Hall & Co.
All rights reserved.
Published by Twayne Publishers
A Division of G. K. Hall & Co.
70 Lincoln Street
Boston, Massachusetts 02111

Copyediting supervised by Barbara Sutton
Book production by Janet Z. Reynolds
Book design by Barbara Anderson

Typeset in 11 pt. Garamond
by Compositors Typesetters, Inc., Cedar Rapids, Iowa

Printed on permanent/durable acid-free paper
and bound in the United States of America

Library of Congress Cataloging-in-Publication Data
Lauber, John, 1925-
    Sir Walter Scott / by John Lauber. — Revised ed.
        p.   cm. — (Twayne's English authors series; TEAS 39)
    Bibliography: p.
    Includes index.
    ISBN 0-8057-6964-1 (alk. paper)
    1. Scott, Walter, Sir, 1771-1832—Criticism and interpretation.
I. Title.   II. Series.
PR5341.L3 1989
828'.709—dc19   88-31270
                                                              CIP

To Jean

CENTRAL ARKANSAS LIBRARY SYSTEM
LITTLE ROCK PUBLIC LIBRARY
100 ROCK STREET
LITTLE ROCK, ARKANSAS 72201

Contents

About the Author

John Lauber holds a doctorate in English from the University of Washington (1957) and has taught at the University of New Mexico and the University of Idaho before joining the faculty of the University of Alberta in 1965, where he is professor of English. His acquaintance with Scott began with a reading of *Ivanhoe* in high school, followed by *The Talisman* as an extracurricular treat. The prose and poetry of early nineteenth-century England has always been one of his primary interests; he has published several essays on the novels of Byron and Jane Austen.

Professor Lauber has written a biography of the young Mark Twain, *The Making of Mark Twain* (1985), as well as papers on Melville, Hawthorne, and Poe. He has combined his interests on Mark Twain and Scott with a paper dealing with Twain's reading, or misreading, of *Ivanhoe* and general critique of the cultural influence of Scott's novels, delivered at a Scott conference held at the University of Alberta. Professor Lauber is the author of essays on the Canadian memoirist and poet John Glassco and on novelist and poet Margaret Atwood. He is now completing a biographical-critical study of Mark Twain.

Preface

Although Scott's novels, inevitably, have lost the mass audience they once attracted, scholarly interest in both his work and his life has greatly increased in the twenty years since the first publication of this book, with the appearance of a new and probably definitive biography, a number of full-length critical studies, and many essays on Scott's individual novels. Not only has the enormous influence of his work on the English novel and on world literature been fully recognized, but across the gap of more than a century and a half, at least some of the Waverley Novels can still speak to us as living works of art.

Scott was a complete man of letters—novelist, poet, critic, historian, biographer, editor—and his total production was enormous. No complete edition of his works has been published, nor is one likely to appear. His scholarly work, however, although important in its own time, has been superseded and can be passed over in a brief study such as this. I devote one chapter in this volume to his poetry, tracing themes and character types that later appeared in his novels, and another to his criticism of fiction, both for its intrinsic interest and for its relation to his own work. The remainder of this study I devoted to his novels.

To write a detailed criticism of each of the thirty-odd Waverley Novels would hardly be practical and, luckily, is unnecessary. The works selected for consideration—*Waverley*, *Guy Mannering*, *The Antiquary*, *Old Mortality*, *Rob Roy*, *The Heart of Midlothian*, *The Black Dwarf*, *A Legend of Montrose*, *The Bride of Lammermoor*, *Ivanhoe*, and *Redgauntlet*—are thoroughly representative and include all the "Scotch novels"—those set in the Scotland of the late seventeenth and eighteenth centuries—which are generally considered Scott's finest. In the concluding chapter certain common characteristics of plot, character, theme, subject, and style are examined and the nature and extent of Scott's influence are considered.

John Lauber

University of Alberta

Chronology

1817   *Harold the Dauntless*, last narrative poem. Beginning of nearly fatal series of attack of gallstones, lasting two years.

1818   *Rob Roy* and *Tales of My Landlord*, second series (*The Heart of Midlothian*). Visited by Washington Irving. Accepts a baronetcy and becomes Sir Walter Scott.

1819   *Tales of My Landlord*, third series (*The Bride of Lammermoor* and *A Legend of Montrose*), and *Ivanhoe*.

1820   *The Monastery, The Abbot*, and *Kenilworth*.

1821   *The Pirate*.

1822   Stage manages visit of George IV to Edinburgh. *The Fortunes of Nigel* and *Peveril of the Peak*.

1823   *Quentin Durward*.

1824   *Redgauntlet* and *St. Ronan's Well*. Completes series of critical biographies of English novelists for the Novelist's Library, published separately as *Lives of the Novelists* (1829).

1825   *Tales of the Crusaders* (*The Talisman* and *The Betrothed*). Commences *Journal*, continued until his death.

1826   Financial ruin. Devotes remainder of his life to paying off his creditors. *Woodstock*.

1827   *Life of Napoleon*, nine volumes.

1828   *The Fair Maid of Perth*.

1829   *Anne of Geierstein*.

1830   *Letters on Demonology and Witchcraft*. Suffers first stroke.

1831   *Count Robert of Paris* and *Castle Dangerous*.

1832   Journey to Italy for health; physical and mental collapse. Scott dies on 21 September at Abbotsford. Leaves "Magnum Opus," revised and annotated edition of his novels, almost completed.

Chapter One
Scott's Literary Career

Walter Scott was born in Edinburgh on 15 August 1771 into a prosperous middle-class family, which still retained close ties with the countryside and the traditions of the Scottish Borders, where the clan of Scotts had been noted for centuries in war, robbery, and feud. The decisive event of his childhood was an attack of infantile paralysis at the age of two, which left him permanently lame because of a shrunken and contracted right leg. In the hope that country air and exercise would restore his health, the child was sent to his grandfather's farm at Smailholme, thirty miles southeast of Edinburgh. Here far more of the Scottish past survived than in bustling, self-consciously enlightened Edinburgh, and the child learned traditional ballads and stories, many of them concerned with the deeds of his own ancestors, and acquired his lifelong love for the countryside and its people. Health and vigor were regained as the boy, in spite of his lameness, grew up to become a tireless walker and a lover of the outdoors; his disability apparently had no such traumatic effect as Lord Byron's club foot. On his return to the city, Scott's education followed the conventional pattern—Edinburgh High School, the University of Edinburgh, training in the law, and admission to the bar in 1792.

First a Poet

Scott, meanwhile, had pursued the interests he had developed as a child. He read widely and indiscriminately—Pope, Dryden, Swift, and Johnson, one assumes, but above all works of romance: Spenser (for the adventures rather than the allegory), *Don Quixote*, the chivalric romances of Ariosto and Boiardo, and Italian poets of the Renaissance. He became a famous storyteller among his schoolmates and improvised with a friend endless tales of knight-errantry. Above all, Scotland's past absorbed him. As a child, he had learned the songs of the Jacobites, supporters of the house of Stuart which had lost the throne of England with the deposition of James II in 1688, and had become a convert to that lost cause. As a boy, he became acquainted with Stewart of Invernahyle, who had fought in the Jacobite rising of 1745, led by the glamorous Bonnie Prince Charlie, who had lain in hiding for weeks on his own estate after the final at Culloden, who had survived a broadsword duel with the famous Highland bandit Rob Roy, and who abounded in tales of Highland life before the clans had been tamed.

Admitted to the bar, Scott practiced with only moderate success, for his interests lay elsewhere. He engaged in an unsuccessful love affair, and made his first experiments in literature. News of the poetry and drama of the German Sturm and Drang movement had reached Edinburgh, and a group of enthusiastic young men, of whom Scott was one, had begun to study the language. The result was the appearance in 1796 of Scott's first published work—translations of the ballads "Lenore" and "Der Wilde Jager" ("The Wild Huntsman") by the German poet Gottfried Bürger—followed in 1799 by a more substantial work, a translation of Goethe's drama, *Götz von Berlichingen*.

None of these works attracted notice. Scott remained a young lawyer who possessed a good deal of leisure time for antiquarian studies, for excursions about the countryside, especially near the Border, to search for ballads and stories, and for practicing literature as an avocation. He had married, but his life was little changed and his relationship with his wife was placid rather than passionate—he never forgot his first love. "Broken-hearted for two years—My heart handsomely pieced again—but the crack will remain till my dying day,"[1] he confided to his journal almost twenty-five years later. But a broken heart (or better still, a cracked one) can be an invaluable asset to a writer.

Meanwhile, he was preparing a major work, *The Minstrelsy of the Scottish Border* (1802). *The Minstrelsy* was a collection of Border ballads, forty-three of them previously unpublished, accompanied by lengthy historical annotation. (Scott was always more interested in ballads as history than as poetry.) Later scholarship has made *The Minstrelsy* obsolete, but the work had a decisive influence on Scott's career. He had discovered his proper subject, Scottish history and tradition, and his first biographer, John Gibson Lockhart, hardly exaggerates in claiming that *The Minstrelsy* was the source of all Scott's later work as poet and novelist.

The Minstrelsy first made Scott's name widely known, but such a work could not be expected to produce much profit. Then, at the suggestion of a friend, he began *The Lay of the Last Minstrel*, a narrative poem including love, war, and sorcery, set on the Scottish Border at the middle of the sixteenth century. Scott's meter, tone, and even occasional phrases were borrowed from Coleridge's "Christabel," which he had heard recited; but since "Christabel" remained unpublished for another ten years, *The Lay* produced an effect of complete originality. Its success was immediate and enormous, and with it Scott became a professional writer.

A second poem promptly followed—*Marmion* (1808)—describing the disastrous battle of Flodden, Scotland's worst defeat in its long wars with England. Its success was even greater. Twenty-five thousand copies were sold within ten years, a sale that would be remarkable in Great Britain of the present day, with a population four times larger. So great had Scott's reputation become that his publisher offered him a thousand pounds for his next work without having seen a line of it. That confidence was justified. *The Lady of the Lake* (1810) made the Highlands fashionable and surpassed the sales of the earlier poems. Scott had made himself the most famous and successful living poet in the English language. Then decline set in with the comparative failure of *Rokeby*, a longer and more complex poem, with a background in the English civil wars. Scott soon recognized that his vogue was expiring and that his poems could not compete with the exotic backgrounds and gloomy intensity of Byron's *Childe Harold* and Eastern tales. He turned to a new field, the novel.

During these years his energies had not been taken up entirely with poetry. Besides his official duties as sheriff of Selkirkshire and clerk of the court, positions that brought him a substantial income while leaving him time and energy for literary work, he had edited complete editions of Dryden and Swift, each prefaced by a full-length biography. These editions do not meet the requirements of modern scholarship, but they remained standard throughout the century. The choice of subject is a significant indication of Scott's literary principles, primarily neoclassic in spite of the superficial romanticism of his subjects and settings.

Businessman and Writer

Scott the lawyer, Scott the editor, and Scott the poet have been considered; Scott the businessman must not be forgotten since his business career had a profound effect on his life and a considerable one on his work. Scott's biographers assure us that he did not really care for money, but he certainly cared intensely for the things money could buy—land, luxury, social position—and the distinction is not easy to make. He strongly believed that authors were exploited by booksellers and wished to earn for himself *all* the profits—those of author, of publisher, and of printer. Accordingly, he entered into a secret partnership with James Ballantyne, owner of a printing shop in Edinburgh.

Secrecy was required because the partnership might have been considered incompatible with Scott's official positions, but he was the dominant partner, controlling every action of the firm and forcing publishers who wanted his own works to have them printed by Ballantyne. (The multivolumed Swift and Dryden editions provided plenty of work.) Soon Ballantyne transformed itself into a publishing house, but that experiment failed disastrously after a few years because of Scott's bad judgment in choosing publications. It was wound up, but left extensive debts and mountainous piles of unsalable volumes.

As the vogue of his poetry passed, it became necessary for Scott either to try a new line or to live on his quite comfortable official income. In this emergency he remembered a fragment of a novel dealing with the Jacobite rising of 1745 that he had written ten years before and had given up when discouraged by the comments of friends. (Scott's picturesque story of accidentally discovering the completely forgotten work while ransacking an old desk in search of fishing tackle need not be accepted; he was methodical in his literary habits and knew very well the potential value of anything he wrote.) The novel, *Waverley*, was completed and published anonymously, in July of 1814, in the usual three-volume form. It took the reading public by storm.

Sales were unprecedented, and the work was read as eagerly in England as in Scotland in spite of the sometimes nearly impenetrable Scots dialect of its minor characters. With its success, Scott had instantly established himself as the great entertainer of his age, admired not only by the general public but by such figures as the prince regent—later George IV—and Byron. The pretense of anonymity was kept up, partly out of a love of mystification and partly from a shrewd calculation that it helped to maintain interest and sales; but all of Scott's contemporaries who counted were aware of the real identity of the author of *Waverley* and its successors. No reader of critical discernment, comparing the novels with Scott's acknowledged works, could have seriously doubted his authorship.

Scott moved quickly to capitalize on his success, exploring the Scottish past in a half-dozen novels written over the next five years, a series that most readers and critics have always considered to be his best work. *Guy Mannering* (1815) and *The Antiquary* (1816) were set in the 1780s and 1790s, respectively, the time of his own childhood and youth. (In only one novel, *St. Ronan's Well* [1824], did he use a contemporary setting. Harshly satirical in its presentation of fashionable or semifashionable life at a Scottish spa, where "medicinal" waters cure imaginary ailments, it is unique among Scott's novels.) *Old Mortality* (1816), the favorite of many readers, presented a conflict of opposing fanaticisms, peasant Presbyterianism and aristocratic royalism, in the Scotland of Charles II. *Rob Roy* (1818) seems a variation on

Waverley, with its return to the Jacobite theme. Again a romantic young Englishman becomes involved in Jacobite plots (this time in 1715), although he never joins the conspirators. *Rob Roy* offered an impetuous heroine, Diana Vernon, who fascinated nineteenth-century readers. Next came a novel that many readers and critics have considered his finest, *The Heart of Midlothian* (1818), unique in Scott's work for its indomitable lower-class heroine, Jeanie Deans, who courageously journeys alone from Edinburgh to London to obtain the queen's pardon for her sister, who is charged with infanticide. Less than a year later *The Heart of Midlothian* was followed by *The Bride of Lammermoor*, Scott's most starkly tragic novel (best known today through Donizetti's *Lucia di Lammermoor*, an operatic adaptation). It was an extraordinary creative outpouring.

That nearly incredible production was necessary. *Waverley* produced immense profits—no earlier writer had approached Scott's earnings—but expenses quickly rose to meet and surpass his new income. Obsessed with the dream of founding a landed family, the Scotts of Abbotsford, and becoming a great "laird" (he had become Sir Walter Scott, baronet, in 1818), living in feudal grandeur surrounded by a devoted peasantry, he recklessly bought hundreds of acres of land at exorbitant prices, planted trees endlessly, built a sham castle complete with turrets and carvings in simulated oak, and stuffed it with armor, weapons, relics, and curios of every sort—spurs worn at the battle of Bannockburn, a cuirass from Waterloo, a lock of hair from the head of Mary Queen of Scots. (Yet Abbotsford incongruously boasted the most modern conveniences, such as water closets and gas lighting.) Each new work paid off old debts and led him to incur new ones, usually to buy more land. Nothing was allowed to interrupt the succession of novels, not even an almost fatal illness. Too weak to hold a pen, Scott dictated *Rob Roy*, and it appeared as scheduled. He did not plan his books, and copy went to the printer as fast as it was written. There is truth, although not the whole truth, in Carlyle's sardonic summary: "Scott's career consisted of writing impromptu novels to buy farms with."[2]

After this long succession of stories with a Scottish background, a change of scene appeared desirable, and Scott set *Ivanhoe* (1819) in the England of Richard the Lion-Hearted, the early thirteenth century, and was rewarded by his greatest success. He exploited English history again in *Kenilworth* (1820), set in the Elizabethan age, and *The Fortunes of Nigel*, notable for its serio-comic portrait of Elizabeth's successor, King James I. *Quentin Durward* (1823), dealing with the fifteenth-century quarrels of King Louis XI of France and Charles the Bold, duke of Burgundy, raised his European fame to a level equal with his English reputation. In 1825 Scott turned to the Crusades with *The Talisman*, notable for its contrast between the humane and enlightened Moslem ruler, Saladin, and the pugnacious, half-barbaric Richard the Lion-Hearted.

Throughout Europe and America, Scott held unchallenged place as the foremost author of the day. But while his earnings were unprecedented, they could not match his spending, and his work showed the strain. Plotting and characterization became more careless, dialogue less natural, situations more repetitious. But once at least, with *Redgauntlet* (1824), he returned to the settings and themes of his early novels and wrote a book that equaled any of them.

Abruptly, Scott's ambitions ended in disaster. Ballantyne had made itself liable for many of Constable's debts, and Constable for Ballantyne, while Scott, as Ballantyne's partner, could be held responsible for both. When the intricate tangle was finally unwound, he found himself owing more than a hundred and twenty thousand pounds—an amount equal to several million dollars today. Ironically, the collapse came only a few months after the long-delayed completion of Abbotsford. Scott could have freed himself from debt through bankruptcy, but he could not bear to sacrifice Abbotsford, and he considered it dishonorable to escape his obligations. Instead, he undertook to pay off the entire amount through his writings.

The remaining six years of his life were given to uninterrupted labor, principally on two massive projects: a nine-volume life of Napoleon (including a full history of the French Revolution), and the "Magnum Opus," a collected edition of his novels, with new prefaces, notes, and revisions. Somehow, he also completed four more novels: *The Fair Maid of Perth* (1828), probably the most successful of this group, offered the novelty of an energetic bourgeois hero as well as a surprisingly subtle and sympathetic study of cowardice, in the character of Conachar, the Highland chief who disgraces himself by fleeing from a battle to the death between rival clans; *Anne of Geierstein* (1829), marked a return to the setting of *Quentin Durward*; and in 1831 *Count Robert of Paris* and *Castle Dangerous*, his last and weakest novels.

By 1831 the debt had been almost cleared, but the strain had been too great, and Scott collapsed, both mentally and physically. The two final novels, *Count Robert of Paris* (1831), set in the Byzantine Empire in the eleventh century, and *Castle Dangerous* (1831), set in fourteenth-century Scotland, clearly show the strain under which they were written. After a useless journey to Italy in search of health, sailing on a warship provided by the British government, Scott came home to die at Abbotsford at the age of sixty-one, on 21 September 1832.

Chapter Two
The Poetry

Scott's poetry appears irretrievably faded today. The long narrative poems on which his poetic reputation depended seem insubstantial in structure and in versification. His language too often alternates between a rather stilted eighteenth-century poetic diction and obtrusive archaisms designed to lend a medieval tone to his work. If Scott survives at all as a poet, it is *The Lady of the Lake* and "Lochinvar"—once high school "standards"—and in a few quotations rapidly losing their familiarity: "Oh, what a tangled web we weave / When first we practice to deceive," "Lives there a man with soul so dead, / Who never to himself hath said, / 'This is my own, my native land'" (*The Lady of the Lake*); "Oh, woman, in our hours of ease, / Uncertain, coy, and hard to please; / When pain and anguish ring the brow, / A ministering angel thou" (*Marmion*).

Yet Scott was a poet for twenty years before he became a novelist, and he continued to be one, if only in the mottoes and songs of the novels, until the end of his career. For six or seven years, from about 1805 to 1812, he was beyond comparison the most widely read and admired of living English poets, and even ten years later it seemed reasonable to Byron, in *Don Juan*, to accord him supremacy over Wordsworth, Coleridge, and Southey, the "Lake poets": "Scott, Rogers, Campbell, Moore and Crabbe will try / 'Gainst thee the question with posterity." Scott's poetry cannot be ignored; it gained him his fame and—more important—in it can be traced the development of the novelist.

Scott's literary career began under the influence of the Sturm and Drang movement, best known for the early work of Goethe, particularly his intensely emotional novel, *The Sorrows of Werther*, and his "Shakespearean" drama of sixteenth-century Germany, *Goetz von Berlichingen*. (Sturm and Drang had already run its course in Germany, but the news reached Scotland late.) Equally important was the propaganda of J. G. Herder for a truly *national* culture. In politically fragmented Germany, that culture could be found only by turning to history and to the people, the *Volk*. Herder collected folk songs, and German poets imitated the folk song and the ballad— although for their ballad models, they turned to an English collection,

8 SIR WALTER SCOTT

Bishop Percy's *Reliques of Ancient English Poetry*. British admirers of Sturm and Drang, in a sense, were simply getting back their own literary tradition, but intensified, exaggerated, melodramatized.

Scott's first publication, in 1796, was a translation of two ballads by Gottfried Bürger, "Lenore" and "Der Wilde Jager" ("The Wild Huntsman"), a horrific tale in which a lost lover returns to his sweetheart at midnight, carries her off to the churchyard, and there reveals himself as a hideous skeleton. The best that can be said of them is that they do not fall far below the level of the originals. But the influence of Bürger was decisive on Scott's development: it directed his attention toward the ballad style and toward the poetic possibilities of traditional lore. It encouraged also a taste for the supernatural—in which he did not often succeed. A translation of *Goetz von Berlichingen* followed three years later.

Reinforcing the influence of Bürger was that of the Scottish popular ballads, which Scott enthusiastically collected, and many of which he had known since childhood. Inevitably, his first original works of any importance, "Glenfinlas" and "The Eve of St. John," were ballad imitations based, like Bürger's work, on legends of terror and the supernatural. Other imitations followed, although, with rare exceptions, Scott could not or did not choose to reproduce the simplicity of diction and the complete objectivity of the best traditional ballads.

Editor of Ballads

Again it appears inevitable, in light of Scott's background and interests, that he should edit a collection of ballads, *The Minstrelsy of the Scottish Border* (three volumes, 1802–3). (Perhaps, too, Scott recognized the chance to make a name for himself; ballads had been fashionable since Bishop Percy's *Reliques of Ancient English Poetry*, published thirty years before.) For such a work, Scott was peculiarly qualified both by study and by early association. He was a "creative" rather than a scrupulous editor, combining different versions of a ballad to make a "standard" text (which had never existed), "correcting" and "improving" the language of the poems—particularly their rhymes—and supplying missing lines, even whole stanzas, and perhaps whole poems—the fine "Twa Corbies" is often attributed to Scott, and if it is really his, will probably prove his most lasting contribution to English poetry.

But Scott cannot be fairly judged by standards of scholarship that did not yet exist. Compared to Percy, who was prepared to include in his *Reliques* anything from "Edward" to Christopher Marlowe's "Come Live with Me and Be My Love," if only it were "antient," he seems a scholarly and systematic editor. He divided his material into three classes: historical ballads, "romantic" ballads, and contemporary imitations (including his own), all accompanied by generous commentary—an eighty-page commentary on popular superstitions, for example, with "Tam Lane."

As an editor, Scott was concerned primarily with the documentary rather than the poetic value of the ballads. Certainly his own poetry suggests that he did not fully recognize the distinctive qualities of the traditional ballads: their simplicity of language, their compression of incident, their perfect objectivity, their tragic intensity. Such a failure of understanding explains his comment that modern imitators were able to supply "elegance of sentiment" and a finished versification that the old ballads lacked, and presumably needed. Yet after all qualifications, *The Minstrelsy* remains a notable work, one of the great ballad collections. It aided the survival of such fine poems as "Lord Randal," "Tam Lane," "The Wife of Usher's Well," and "The Demon Lover."

The Lay of the Last Minstrel

So scholarly and expensive a work as *The Minstrelsy* could hardly become a best-seller ("It was, on the whole, one of those books which are more praised than they are read," Scott observed in his introduction to a later edition), but it established its editor's reputation. Ready for more ambitious original work, Scott soon carried out his desire to present the "manners" of the old Scottish Border on a larger scale than a ballad would permit. Accident provided him with a subject when the countess of Dalkeith suggested a poem dealing with a Border legend of a goblin page and his malicious pranks. Another accident gave Scott his verse form, when he heard a friend who was familiar with the poetry of Wordsworth and Coleridge recite aloud parts of Coleridge's still unpublished "Christabel." "The form of 'Christabel,'" Scott remarked in his introduction, "from the singularly irregular structure of the stanzas, and the liberty which it allowed the author to adapt the sound to the sense, seemed exactly suited to such an extravaganza as I meditated."

The composition of *The Lay* was thoroughly characteristic of its author in the speed with which it was composed and in its departure from his original plan. When the poem outgrew his intention of a few stanzas about a goblin page, Scott wrote on with no idea of how *The Lay* was to end. Like most of his work, the poem was composed at a breakneck pace, a canto a week. Its most distinctive feature, the "frame" provided by the aged minstrel who recites the story almost a century and a half after it had supposedly taken place, resulted from the suggestion of friends that a prologue was needed to put the reader in the proper frame of mind. The final result was an extremely confused narrative of love and war, of sorcery and goblin pranks, set on the Scottish

Border—the ancestral territory of the Scotts—in the mid–sixteenth century, with a dash of pathos added in the character of the last minstrel.

Scott had expected success, but not the enormous popularity *The Lay* instantly won. "In the history of British poetry," wrote Lockhart thirty years later, "nothing has ever equalled the demand for *The Lay of the Last Minstrel*."[1] The figures support his claim—at least 44,000 copies sold before Scott's death in 1832. Given the high cost of books and the relatively small population of England and Scotland at the time, such a sale indicates that the early nineteenth century, unlike the twentieth, was a poetry-reading age.

But the comparison is not quite so much to the disadvantage of the present as it might seem. The popular poetry of Scott's day, whether by himself, or Byron, or Crabbe, or Moore, was narrative poetry, usually neither subtle nor complex, and nearly as easy to read as a novel—much easier than many modern novels. More original and demanding works, such as the poems of Wordsworth and Keats, sold by the hundreds, or the dozens. The public for Scott's verse was the entertainment-seeking one that today is amused by television, the movies, or best-selling novels. The audience for difficult poetry may have been no larger, proportionately, in 1805 or 1810 than it is today.

Faults of structure were obvious and freely admitted by the author. As the poem developed, the goblin page had become, in Scott's word, an "excrescence," and the whole sixth canto, describing the festivities at the wedding of the hero and heroine, and containing the songs of the minstrels, was unnecessary. But, as Scott explained in a letter to a friend, "the poem should certainly have closed with the union of the lovers, when the interest, if any, was at an end. But what could I do? I had my book and my page still on my hands, and must get rid of them. . . . Manage them as I would, their catastrophe must have been insufficient to occupy an entire canto; so I was fain to eke it out with the songs of the minstrels."[2]

Readers, however, were entranced by the apparent novelty of subject and form, and they agreed with a reviewer who observed that "delightful images and affecting sentiments" were more important than unity or coherence. Luckily, too, "Christabel" was unavailable for comparison. Coleridge's description of Christabel's entry into her father's castle with the mysterious Geraldine can be matched with Scott's account of his heroine going forth at night to meet her lover:

"Christabel"

The mastiff old did not awake
Yet she an angry moan did make!

. . . .
They passed the hall, that echoes still,
Pass as lightly as you will!
The brands wee flat, the brands were dying,
Amid their own white ashes lying:

. . . .
They steal their way from stair to stair,
Now in glimmer and now in gloom,
And now they pass the Baron's room
As still as death, with stifled breath!

The Lay of the Last Minstrel

Why does she stop and look often around,
    As she glides down the secret stair;
And why does she pat the shaggy bloodhound
    As he rouses him up from his lair?
And, though she passes the postern alone,
    Why is not the watchman's bugle blown?
The ladye steps in doubt and dread
    Lest her watchful mother hear her tread;
The ladye caresses the rough bloodhound
    Lest his voice should waken the castle round.

Coleridge was justifiably disturbed, not so much by the obvious plagiarism—Scott is not saved by the fact that his heroine is leaving a castle while Coleridge's is entering one—as by the manner in which Scott coarsened the passage, making language and meter heavy and obvious. The subtleties of the "Christabel" meter were beyond Scott's capacity, and by canto 3 the poem settles into the rather irregular iambic tetrameter couplets that became typical of his longer poems. Modern readers will probably agree with Grierson that "in the best of the ballads, say 'Tamlane' and 'The Twa Corbies,' there is more of imaginative poetry than in the whole of *The Lay*."[3] But whatever its poetic qualities, *The Lay* established Scott as an original writer, rather than a translator and editor, and won him the audience that he would never lose.

Marmion

With the publication of *The Lay*, literature rather than law became Scott's real profession. So brilliant a success had to be followed up, but Scott was delayed by the variety of literary tasks he had undertaken, and as a result

Marmion did not appear until 1808. The author intended, the introductory advertisement to the poem announced, "to paint the manners of the feudal times upon a broader scale, and in the course of a more interesting story" than in *The Lay*. The frame provided by the character of the last minstrel, supposedly singing Scott's poem, was replaced by a series of introductory epistles—one preceding each canto—describing the scenery and seasons of Ashestiel, Scott's residence at the time of writing, and containing the author's meditations on poetry and many other subjects. (It was thoroughly characteristic of Scott that these verse-letters, which now seem the most attractive parts of *Marmion*, were originally composed to appear independently as "Six Epistles from Ettrick Forest.")

The poem reaches its climax with the great national disaster of Flodden, fought in 1513, in which almost the entire Scottish army, including King James IV and most of his nobility, was annihilated by the English. The narrative, however, is concerned with the adventures of purely fictitious characters whose fates are determined by the outcome of the historical battle—a method later typical of Scott's novels. Lord Marmion, a favorite of Henry VIII, journeys to Scotland to inquire about the warlike preparations of King James. Marmion has previously sought the hand of an heiress, the beautiful Clara de Clare. Clara is in love with Ralph de Wilton, but Marmion disposes of his rival by forging a letter implicating him in treason, then by overthrowing him in a trial by battle. Clara takes refuge in a nunnery; De Wilton (who survives the trial by combat) wanders in disguise and finally guides Marmion (who of course does not recognize him) to Edinburgh. Meanwhile, wishing to be free to marry Clara, Marmion has betrayed his mistress, Constance de Beverley, whom he had stolen from a convent. In punishment for violating her oath of chastity, Constance is immured alive, but first produces documents proving De Wilton's innocence. Finally, Marmion is killed at Flodden and De Wilton is united with Clara.

As would become usual in Scott's works, the official hero and heroine are the least interesting characters in the work. No reader could feel much concern over whether Clara will be forced to marry Marmion, or how De Wilton will regain his reputation. Marmion is more interesting—dark, proud, haunted by guilt, the first complete Byronic hero in English literature, at a time when Byron had published nothing but his juvenile *Hours of Idleness*. Violent, passionate, continuously drawing the reader's attention away from the official hero, Marmion is the first of a succession of "dark heroes," as they have been named by Alexander Welsh, in Scott's poems and later in his novels.

Francis Jeffrey, in the *Edinburgh Review*, pointed out that the story was inadequate for a poem of such length, and that it seemed "to turn upon a tissue of incredible accidents"; he protested against "the insufferable number, and length and minuteness" of Scott's descriptions of ancient costumes and manners and buildings, of ceremonies and superstitions, and concluded that to write a romance of chivalry in the early nineteenth century "seems to be as much a fantasy as to build a modern abbey, or an English pagoda";[4] but the public disagreed. The success of *Marmion* equaled that of *The Lay*, and totally disproved Jeffrey's prophecy that Scott must either sacrifice his Border prejudices, or offend his English readers. At least one contemporary in addition to Jeffrey remained immune to the spell; Wordsworth, in a letter to Scott, remarked dryly that "I think your end has been attained. That it is not the end which I should wish you to propose to yourself, you will be well aware."[5] But Scott finished his introduction to *Marmion* in the collected edition of his works by complacently noting that "the return of sales before me makes the copies amount to thirty-six thousand printed between 1808 and 1825."

The Lady of the Lake

The Lady of the Lake (1810) achieved the greatest popularity of all of Scott's poems. Suspense was aroused long before the poem's appearance, as James Ballantyne, the printer, read cantos aloud to selected listeners. "Common fame was loud in their favor," a contemporary reported. "A great poem was on all hands anticipated. I do not recollect that any of all the author's works was ever looked for with more intense anxiety, or that any of them excited a more extraordinary sensation when it did appear." Scott's poem had made the Highlands a tourist attraction. "Crowds set off to view the scenery of Loch Katrine . . . and every house and inn in that neighborhood was crammed with a constant succession of visitors."[6]

Again, the historical background is that of pre-Reformation Scotland, but this time the action occurs in the Highlands rather than on the Border. The distinctive peculiarities of the earlier poems reappear. The official hero, Malcolm Graeme, is as insignificant as Ralph de Wilton, and again the reader's interest is usurped by a "dark hero"—Roderich Vich Alpine Dhu, Highland chieftain and robber. As in *The Lay*, the final canto, with its description of a battle between Highlanders and Lowlanders, is superfluous. As Scott admitted, "all the principal characters had been disposed of . . . and were absent at the time of action, and nothing hinged upon the issue."[7] But the public did not care; it was delighted by the picturesque scenery of the Highlands and the still more picturesque manners and customs of the Highlanders.

One dissent was registered in private by the best critic of the time. Writing
to Wordsworth after reading the first two cantos, Coleridge complained of
the slowness of movement, both of the verse and action, and proposed a formula for such poems: "The first business must be, a vast string of Patronym-
ics, and names of Mountains, Rivers, etc.—the most commonplace imagery
. . . look almost as well as new by the introduction of Benroirlich, Namvar, or
copse-wood Gray that *moaned and wept on Loch Achray* and mingled with the
pine-trees *blue* on the bold cliffs of Ben Venue. . . . Second all the nomencla-
ture of Gothic architecture, of Heraldry, of Arms, of Hunting and Falconry
. . . they will stand by themselves, stout substantives, if only they are strung
together, and some attention is paid to the sound of the words—for no one
attempts to understand the meaning, which indeed would snap the charm
. . . some pathetic moralizing on old times, or anything else, for the head and
tail pieces—with a *Bard* (that is absolutely necessary) and Songs of course."
Characters and episodes could be borrowed from the Gothic novels of Ann
Radcliffe, with the advantage that "however threadbare in the Romance
shelves of the circulating Library," they will seem "quite new as soon as told in
rhyme."[8]

Decline of the Poetry

With *The Lady of the Lake*, Scott's poetic career had reached its climax.
The decline was immediate. The next poem, *Rokeby*, (1813), set in England
during the civil wars of the seventeenth century, sold respectably but failed to
match the sensational success of the earlier poems. *The Bridal of Triermain*
(1813), published anonymously, and *The Lord of the Isles* (1815), dealing
with Scotland's national hero, Robert the Bruce, were even less successful.
Scott's poetry had lost its freshness, parodists and imitators had appeared,
and he had been surpassed by a new competitor, Byron.

The poetry of Scott, Coleridge predicted, would not survive, and his
prophecy has been verified. A contemporary admirer, John Adolphus, provides one of the fullest descriptions of its characteristics—a description that
helps to explain both the instant popularity of the earlier poems and their
lack of permanent interest. Writing in 1822, Adolphus describes the style as
"popular," possessing an "easy openness . . . expanded, simple and consecu-
tive." Scott prefers simile to metaphor (a frequent source of difficulty to readers of poetry); he avoids apparently illogical associations and compressed
descriptions. Adolphus quotes Shakespeare's lines from *Henry V*: "Now en-
tertain conjecture of a time / When creeping murmur and the poring dark /
Fill the wide corner of the universe . . . ." Nowhere, he adds, does Scott

"adopt this kind of poetical phraseology, which conveys in a few words the germ and essence of a beautiful or sublime description, but is not itself that description." Unlike the poetry of Wordsworth, Coleridge, Keats, Shelley, or Blake, Scott's verse was as easy to read as prose. Unlike them also, he shared the tastes and attitudes of the reading public. As Adolphus puts it, "his verse is not the expression of sentiments cherished, and speculations prosecuted, by a refined and fanciful individual, but the lively copy of those sensations and habits of mind" that are shared by "the generality of mankind."[9]

Verse came easily to Scott. The poems were rapidly written and were meant to be rapidly read. For such reading, it was enough if the author simply named the poetic objects—bards, knights, ladies, castles, crags, swords, spears. Readers could be trusted to respond. "To form an estimate of Scott's poetry," Coleridge remarked, it would be necessary to "take away all his names of old castles, which rhyme very prettily, and read very picturesquely; then . . . all the old armour and weapons; next I would exclude the mention of all nunneries, abbeys, and priories, and then I should see what would be the residuum—how much poetry would remain."[10] Very little, is the clear implication.

But Scott's poetry was an essential preparation for his novels, and in that fact lies its real interest. With *The Lay of the Last Minstrel*, he had become admittedly an imaginative writer, a writer of fictional narrative, rather than a scholar and editor. Yet *The Lay*, like its successors, was heavily annotated, with detailed explanations of archaic terms and customs and of geographical and historical references. The scholarly apparatus, the introductions and notes and glossaries that Scott would provide for both his poems and his novels, "seem almost," as a modern critic has observed, "to derive from an uneasiness on Scott's part with poetry in its naked condition" as purely imaginative, purely fictional . . . detached from the world of rational discourse. The apparatus looks like an attempt to contextualize and explain, to ground the world of the imagination in that of actual history and geography and so render it 'safe' . . . to detach Walter Scott, Esq. from the troubling figure of the poetic creator."[11]

The Lay and its successors reveal also the importance that Scott placed throughout his career on locality and local or regional identity, and on the continuity of past and present. But such concerns and such interests could be expressed more fully in novels than in narrative poems—a fact that the first readers of the Waverley Novels realized. Scott had prepared his audience.

Chapter Three
The Art of Fiction

Although Scott devoted only a fraction of his effort to criticism, and only a fraction of his criticism to the novel, even that surpasses—in both quantity and importance—the work of any previous or contemporary critic of fiction. His published criticism is found in reviews of current novels, in the series of critical biographies prefaced to the British novelists series and later collected as *Lives of the Novelists*, and in the prefaces and introductions to his own novels. His journal and his letters provide informal comments on his contemporaries and, together with the introductions to the novels, illustrate the relation between his critical principles and his own practice as a creative writer.

Fiction—A Luxury

Basic to both criticism and practice is Scott's opinion of the novel as a minor literary form, "a mere elegance, a luxury contrived for the amusement of polished life and the gratification of that half-love of literature which pervades all ranks in an advanced state of society."[1] He defends it against the attacks of moralists by denying its significance. He does not share the romantic belief in the power of the creative imagination to create or reveal truth. Fiction, for him, is make-believe, simply providing amusement. The function of the novel is to offer "solace from the toils of ordinary life by an excursion into the regions of imagination"; it is a drug, harmful to the addict, but "of most blessed power in those moments when the whole head is sore and the whole heart sick."[2] He refuses to take his own work seriously; his references to it, as in his prefaces, are humorous, self-deprecatory, self-exposing.

The natural consequence of this attitude is an indifference to the artistic qualities of the novel that is abundantly revealed by Scott's own methods of work. *Guy Mannering* was "the work of six weeks at Christmas."[3] "Before and after dinner I finished about twenty printed pages of *Woodstock*,"[4] and in fifteen days "with intervention of some days idleness, to let imagination brood on the task a little,"[5] Scott completed a volume. Such speed allowed little revision and no planning at all. Finishing the second volume of *Woodstock*, Scott found himself with no idea of how the story was to be concluded, and observed that "I never could lay down a plan—or, having laid it down, I never could adhere to it . . . . I only tried to make that which I was actually writing diverting and interesting, leaving the rest to fate."[6]

Scott saw himself not as an artist but as a craftsman supplying a luxury product, demand for which might cease at any moment. His remark on the comparative failure of his narrative poem, "The Lord of the Isles"—"Since one line has failed, we must just stick to something else"[7]—suggests a manufacturer withdrawing an obsolescent product in order to replace it with a new model. To vary the metaphor, his novels were the bricks with which Abbotsford was built. Shortly after the crash of Ballantyne and Constable and his own financial ruin, he lamented in his journal that "I can no longer have the delight of waking in the morning with bright ideas in my mind, haste to commit them to paper, and count them monthly, as the means of planting such groves, and purchasing such wastes."[8] Like a good showman, Scott sought for novelty—Highlanders, Covenanters, Crusaders, fifteenth-century France, Anglo-Norman England—until only one source remained: "to depend for success on the interest of a well-contrived story. But woe's me! That requires thought, consideration, the writing out of a regular plan or plot,"[9] and of that Scott believed himself incapable.

For the public that consumed the output of his literary production line, Scott felt a certain contempt. The public, he remarks in his journal, is amused with "rattles and gingerbread" and cannot discriminate: "I should deal very uncandidly with those who may read my confessions were I to say I knew a public worth caring for . . . . Get a good name and you may write trash. Get a bad one and you may write like Homer, without pleasing a single reader."[10]

Criticism

Works produced in such a way, for such a public, would hardly deserve very serious or detailed study. As a result, Scott's criticism of fiction is descriptive and impressionistic rather than analytical. Thus, after praising in general terms the plot of *Tom Jones* (in his life of Fielding), instead of examining its construction, Scott falls back on simile to suggest its effect on the reader, who "glides down the narrative like a boat on the surface of some broad navigable stream, which only winds enough to gratify the voyager with the varied beauty of its banks."[11]

His review of Jane Austen's *Emma* is typical of his approach. Beginning with a brief discussion of the novel as a literary form, he derives it from the "romance," then distinguishes two contrasting types. "The novel as formerly composed" was characterized by improbability of action and exaggeration of sentiment; but a new type of fiction has appeared "which draws the characters and incidents introduced more immediately from the current of ordinary life than was permitted by the former rules of the novel,"[12] and to this class *Emma* belongs.

With *Emma* properly classified, Scott sums up its merits: "the force of a narrative conducted with much neatness and point, and a quiet yet comic dialogue, in which the characters of the speakers evolve themselves with dramatic effect."[13] He praises characterization, dialogue, and description, then remarks, oddly, that *Emma* has almost no story—Scott apparently conceives of "story" as a succession of adventures. He nevertheless summarizes the plot at length and concludes condescendingly, "Such is the simple plan of a story which we peruse with pleasure, if not with deep interest."[14]

He later came to realize the uncommon qualities of Jane Austen's apparently commonplace realism. "That young lady had a talent for describing the involvements and feelings and characters of ordinary life which is to me the most wonderful I ever met with," he observed in his journal in 1826. "The Big Bow-wow strain I can do myself like any now going but the exquisite touch which renders ordinary common-place things and characters interesting from the truth of the description and the sentiment is denied to me."[15] And a year later he observed simply that "there is a truth of painting in her writings which always delights me."[16]

His review of Mary Shelley's *Frankenstein* (1818) begins in a similar manner, with a distinction between novels that "bound the events they narrate by the actual laws of nature, and such as, passing these limits are managed by marvellous and supernatural machinery." Works presenting the "marvellous" are further subdivided into three classes: those written in a time when there was genuine belief in the supernatural and miraculous (like the ballads he collected); those that present supernatural events merely for their sensational effect (like the sensational Gothic novels of his own time); and, finally, a "more philosophical and refined" class "in which the laws are represented as altered . . . in order to show the probable effect which the supposed miracles would produce on those who witnessed them."[17] *Frankenstein* belongs to this highest class.

Without quite recognizing the distinctive quality of *Frankenstein*, probably the first science-fiction novel in the modern sense, Scott nevertheless describes the unique satisfaction provided to the reader by such works, in which "the pleasure derived from the marvellous incidents is secondary to that which we extract from observing how mortals like ourselves would be effected." However fantastic the basic situation may be, the implied contract between author and reader requires that the characters should behave "ac-

cording to the rules of probability and the nature of the human heart."
Frankenstein, then, displays "uncommon powers of poetic imagination," and
in conclusion Scott congratulates readers on receiving "a novel which excites
new reflections and untried sources of emotion."[18] For a review from the conservative Scott, published in the ferociously Tory *Blackwood's*, the judgment
is surprisingly favorable. (*Frankenstein* was dedicated to the radical philosopher William Godwin, and Scott believed that it was written by Shelley himself, a notorious "atheist.")

Scott is anything but a systematic or theoretical critic, but his basic concept
of literature is clearly and firmly neoclassic: literature is an imitation of life.
(Scott actually applies the term to his own work in his prefatory remark that
St. Ronan's Well "is intended to give the imitation of the shifting manners of
our time." "By the circumstantial detail of minute, trivial, and even uninteresting circumstances," he notes, "the author gives to his fiction an air of reality
that can scarcely otherwise be obtained."[19] Although his terminology differs
widely, Scott anticipates the observation of a modern literary historian that
"formal realism," defined as the convention that "the novel is a full and au-
thentic report of human experience, and is therefore under an obligation to
satisfy its reader with such details of the story as the individuality of the actors
concerned, the particulars of the times and places of their actions, details that
are presented through a more largely referential use of language than is common in other literary forms,"[20] is the defining characteristic of the form. It
was just such "particulars" of actions occurring in distant times and places
that delighted Scott's own readers.

Chapter Four
Waverley

Scott's career as novelist began late (he was forty-two when *Waverley* appeared and, according to his own account, almost by accident, resulting from the chance discovery of a fragment of manuscript and from the declining popularity of his poems and the rising fame of Byron. In fact, however, Scott's whole life pointed toward the novel. From his childhood he had displayed a love of storytelling. As a boy he had been able to amuse himself and his schoolmates for hours at a time with improvised tales of chivalry; as an adult, his conversational ability lay in anecdote, for which he was famous, rather than in repartee or disputation.

Scott was always an enthusiastic novel reader, and it was natural enough that some of his first literary experiments should be in this form. Two fragments composed before 1800 have survived. The longer and more interesting, *Thomas the Rhymer*, was intended to be "a tale of chivalry . . . in the style of *The Castle of Otranto*, with plenty of Border characters and supernatural incident"[1]—a kind of prose equivalent, in fact, of *The Lay of the Last Minstrel*. *Thomas*, like its companion piece *The Lord of Ennerdale*, never advanced beyond the opening chapter; but Scott did not lose interest in the novel.

Still another experiment followed, this time to be published—Scott's completion of Joseph Strutt's *Queenhoo Hall* (1808), a historical novel set in fifteenth-century England. Strutt, a famous antiquarian, had made his book almost unreadable by its profusion of historical detail. From its failure Scott learned a useful lesson: "by rendering his language too ancient, and displaying his antiquarian knowledge too liberally, the ingenious author had raised up an obstacle to his own success. Every work designed for mere amusement must be expressed in language easily comprehended."[2] ("Mere amusement"—that phrase sums up Scott's attitude toward his own work, both his narrative poems and his novels.) It was unnecessary and undesirable, Scott believed, to reproduce literally the language of a bygone age; it was enough to avoid obvious anachronisms, to suggest the general tone or style of a period, and perhaps to season the dialogue with an occasional archaism.

At about the same time, Scott had begun *Waverley* and completed seven chapters. The exact date of composition cannot be determined since his own account, given many years later in the general preface to the Waverley Novels, is self-contradictory. "My early recollections of the Highland scenery and customs made so favourable an impression in the poem called the Lady of the Lake," Scott wrote, "that I was induced to think of attempting something of the same kind in prose. It was with some idea of this kind, that, about the year 1805, I threw together about one-third part of the first volume of Waverley."[3] But the date of 1805 is impossible since *The Lady of the Lake* was not published until 1810. What is certain is that Waverley was advertised in a list of forthcoming books for 1809–10. But when Scott asked the opinion of friends about the book, they unanimously condemned it and *Waverley* was put aside. When Scott finally returned to it, he finished it with almost unbelievable speed, writing the last two volumes in three weeks. *Waverley, or 'Tis Sixty years Since* was published anonymously in July 1814. The author's motive for anonymity, according to his own later statement in his general preface to the collected edition of his novels, was simply his consciousness that the book was "an experiment in the public taste" that could easily fail.

Waverley, then, was left to make its way without help from its author's name, and quickly did so. The time was propitious. Napoleon had abdicated a few months before and was now exiled in Elba, peace had apparently returned after more than twenty years of continuous war, and England had not only survived but had won a glorious victory and considered itself the savior of Europe from revolutionary chaos and Napoleonic tyranny. Patriotic readers were in a mood to explore the past that had made England what it was, and to recognize Scottish history as a part of a common British heritage.

Considering all of these preliminary attempts, recognizing the steady development in his work toward longer and more complex narrative, the surprising fact is not that Scott finally became a novelist but that he waited so long to do so. The delay may be explained in part by the comparatively low prestige of the novel in his time and by the fact that verse was still considered the natural medium for narrative. (Not only Byron, but Wordsworth, Coleridge, Shelley, Keats, and Crabbe wrote narrative poems.) If Scott had been born a contemporary of Dickens rather than of Wordsworth, he surely would have turned directly to the novel, and might never have written poetry at all.

Critical Reception

The year 1814 seems in retrospect a notable one in the history of English literature, for it witnessed the publication not only of *Waverley* but of Wordsworth's *Excursion* (an intensely unpopular work except among a small sect of disciples) and of Jane Austen's *Mansfield Park* (which enjoyed substantial but not sensational popularity). To contemporaries, however, *Waverley* overshadowed everything else. Only one reviewer, John Wilson Croker, was positively hostile. Croker pronounced dogmatically in the *Quarterly Review* that "we have a great objection . . . to historical romance, in which real and fictitious personages and actual fabulous events are mixed together to the utter confusion of the reader and the unsettling of all accurate recollections of past transaction"[4] (a judgment that would have damned Shakespeare's history plays and Roman tragedies along with *Waverley*) and wished that Scott had written a history of the Jacobite rising of 1745 instead of a novel.

More typical of critical opinion was the judgment of the *Edinburgh Review*, which found *Waverley* full of "nature and truth," so much so that its scenes and characters must have been "copied from existing originals."[5] But the public did not wait for reviewers to praise or blame. "Except for the first opening of the *Edinburgh Review*," wrote one reader, "no work that has appeared in my time made such an instant and universal impression . . . . The unexpected newness of the thing, the profusion of original characters, the Scotch language, Scotch scenery, Scotch men and women, the simplicity of the writing, and the graphic force of the descriptions, all struck us with an electric shock of delight . . . . If the concealment of the authorship was intended to make mystery heighten their effect, it succeeded. The speculations and conjectures, and nods and winks, and predictions and assertions were endless, and occupied every company, and almost every two men who met and spoke in the street."[6]

The odds might have seemed to be against *Waverley*—a work "hastily" and "unskilfully" written, as one critic observed, largely composed in a dialect "unintelligible to four-fifths of the reading population of the country" and "relating to a period too recent to be romantic, and too far gone by to be familiar."[7] But the public bought and read, undeterred by thickets of dialogue in broad Scots. The enthusiasm was unprecedented, and the publisher, Constable, could not keep up with the demand. "We have this moment finished *Waverley*," wrote Maria Edgeworth, herself a novelist. "It was read aloud to this large family, and I wish the author could have witnessed the impression it made—the strong hold it seized of the feelings both of young and old—the admiration raised by the beautiful descriptions of nature—by the new and bold delineations of character—the perfect manner in which character is sustained in every change of situation . . . the ingenuity with which each person introduced . . . is made useful and necessary to the end . . . ."[8] For two generations at least, that experience would be repeated as the Waverley Novels, as Scott's novels soon came to be called, were read aloud in countless thousands of homes throughout the English-speaking world.

Scott might have foreseen the popularity of *Waverley* in Scotland; but he could hardly have predicted that the English audience would delight equally in Scotch scenery, characters, and even language. The English success of *Waverley* was so unprecedented that it prompted Jane Austen's humorous complaint that "Walter Scott has no business to write novels, especially good ones—It is not fair. He has fame and profit enough as a poet and should not be taking the bread out of other people's mouths. I do not mean to like *Waverley* if I can help it—but I fear I must."[9] (Obviously the authorship was no secret to discerning readers.)

Many causes contributed to the popularity of the Waverley Novels, but one of the most important surely was "the unexpected newness of the thing." *Waverley* was original in its presentation of regional peculiarities[10]—"Scotch language, Scotch scenery, Scotch men and women"—which in eighteenth-century fiction had appeared only as subjects for ridicule when they were presented at all. Particularly, of course, Highland characters and "manners" were strikingly fresh and picturesque. There was little wonder that the work appealed to a public that was becoming bored with Gothic terrors. *Waverley* was new too in its use of history (though Scott had always the precedent of Shakespeare's history plays in mind); in fact, it can justifiably be called the first historical novel. Historical forgeries like Defoe's *Journal of the Plague Year* could hardly be considered novels, and Gothic novels, although vaguely medieval in their settings, were completely unhistorical.

Structure

The opening six chapters, however, provided a barrier high enough to test any reader's enthusiasm. Presenting Waverley's education, tastes, family history, and the political background against which he was raised, they supply essential information but are completely undramatic; they consist almost entirely of exposition that is interrupted occasionally by the author's commentary. Admitting their dullness, Scott claimed that he had "left the story to flag in the first volume on purpose . . . to avoid the usual error of novel writers, whose first volume is usually their best,"[11] an explanation that sounds remarkably like a rationalization. No writer as concerned with sales as Scott would have deliberately chosen to bore his readers through a whole volume. Scott, however, exaggerated by saying that the whole first volume was made dull; with Waverley's arrival at Tully-Veolan, in Chapter 8, his true story commences.

Neglected by his father, an ambitious politician, Edward Waverley has been brought up by his rich and elderly uncle, Sir Everard Waverley. Left much to himself, he (like the young Walter Scott) reads widely in poetry and romance, creating an imaginary world of poetry and romance that he much prefers to the prosaic present. Like Jane Austen's Catherine Morland in *Northanger Abbey*, he is the victim of an undisciplined imagination. Unlike Catherine, he will discover through experience that the adventures he dreams of are real, and that the hardship, pain, and danger they involve are highly disagreeable. The role of romantic adventurer, devoting his sword to a doomed cause, is more pleasant to imagine than to experience.

Waverley's politics, as far as he has any, are influenced more strongly by the old-fashioned Toryism of his uncle and his tutor than by his father's opportunistic loyalty to George II and the ruling Whigs. Sir Everard is at least a theoretical Jacobite, but sympathy for the house of Stuart does not prevent Sir Everard from choosing a military career, in support of the existing government, for his nephew, and young Waverley is dispatched to join a regiment in Scotland. Bored with his duties, he visits the Baron of Bradwardine, his uncle's old friend, at the Baron's estate of Tully-Veolan at the foot of the Highlands. Here the real action of the novel commences, as Waverley seems to be actually entering the world of romance. The clock of history has been turned back, for the Baron is a feudal lord ruling and caring for his devoted tenants. He even keeps a Shakespearean fool, the half-crazed Davie Gellatly, who communicates more by music than by words. (But the price of romance is shown to be ignorance and poverty.) A staunch keeper of old traditions, the Baron is a Jacobite as well, who has already risked life and fortune in the unsuccessful rising of 1715 and is ready to try again to overturn the ruling house of Hanover.

Visiting the great hall of the clan Mac-Ivor at Glennaquoich in the neighboring Highlands, Waverley seems to be penetrating still further into the romantic past—here a living present. He sees a patriarchal society where chieftain and follower feast together, united by ties of kinship rather than feudal law, not recognizing that Fergus deliberately revives and encourages such traditions in order to increase his own authority. Glennaquoich, with its Homeric bard chanting war songs,is in part an artificial creation. Naively overlooking these realities, Waverley is dominated by the fiery energy of Fergus and captivated by the beauty of his sister, Flora, and is deeply influenced by their fanatical enthusiasm for the Jacobite cause, so much more romantic than loyalty to the dull George II.

Meanwhile, Prince Charles Stuart, the "Young Pretender" of his enemies and "Bonnie Prince Charlie" of his friends, has landed to reclaim the throne for his family. By accident and force of circumstance, Waverley is forced into joining the Prince's cause. He falls under suspicion because of his prolonged visits to Bradwardine and Fergus, both notorious Jacobites, his return is delayed by a hunting accident, letters recalling him to his regiment are intercepted by the robber Donald Bean Lean, and he is relieved of his command. He becomes a nearly helpless victim of circumstance, as Scott's heroes will often be.

Returning to assert his innocence, Waverley is arrested, then rescued and held prisoner—by whom, he does not know—and finally brought to Edinburgh, now held by the Jacobites. Common sense tells him that the rebellion is hopeless and that in any case it is not worth bringing civil war into a peaceful country merely to change kings, but he seems to have no alternative. Carried away by romantic enthusiasm and the personal charm of Prince Charles, by hope of winning Flora's love, and by the dominating personality of Fergus, he pledges himself to the Prince's service and is present at the Jacobite victory of Preston-pans, where instead of striking a blow, he saves the life of an English officer, Colonel Talbot. The Scott hero is typically nonviolent.

When the Jacobite invasion of England fails, Waverley is separated from the retreating army and forced into hiding. Eventually, through the influence of Colonel Talbot, who has been released on parole, he gains a pardon. After witnessing the trial and condemnation of Fergus, though not his terrible death, he marries Rose Bradwardine (after Flora has more than once decisively rejected him) and restores the Baron's confiscated estates to their owner, while Flora disappears into a French convent. This marriage to the sweet and simple Rose, instead of the powerful and dominating Flora, also sets a pattern for the future novels. Bailie Macwheeble's exultation clearly at the news—"Lady Waverley! ten thousand a year, the least penny!—Lord preserve my poor understanding!"—seems a deliberate echo of Mrs. Bennet's frantic excitement, in Jane Austen's *Pride and Prejudice*, on learning that Elizabeth is engaged to Darcy: "Ten thousand a year! Oh Lord! What will become of me! I shall go distracted."

As for Waverley's future, it has been accurately prophesied by Flora: a "quiet circle of domestic happiness, lettered indolence, and elegant enjoyments, of Waverley-Honour," his uncle's estate. There, "He will refit the old library in the most exquisite Gothic taste . . . and he will draw plans and landscapes, and write verses, and rear temples, and dig grottoes;—and he will stand in a clear summer night . . . and gaze on the deer as they stray in the moonlight, or lie shadowed by the boughs of the huge old fantastic oaks;— and he will repeat verses to his beautiful wife, who will hang upon his arm." It is a future entirely appropriate to Waverley's character, yet its ease and comfort inevitably seem trivial in comparison to the terrible realities he has witnessed.

Finally, the author accounts for the disappearance of the letters and Waverley's mysterious imprisonment with a naive explanation: "These circumstances will serve to explain such points of our narrative as, according to the custom of storytellers, we deemed it fit to leave unexplained, for the purpose of exciting the reader's curiosity."

Such a plot is obviously "inartificial," to use Scott's own term, and perhaps the best comment on it is provided by the author himself in his preface: "The tale of Waverley was put together with so little care, that I cannot boast of having sketched any distinct plan of the work. The whole adventures of Waverley, in his movements up and down the country with the Highland cateran Bean Lean, are managed without much skill. It suited best, however, the road I wanted to travel, and permitted me to introduce some description of scenery and manners." Plot, for him, was primarily a means for bringing in whatever persons, events, or scenes he wished to describe. He never attempted, and was probably incapable of, a well-made plot like that of *Tom Jones.* That "inartificiality" disturbed few if any readers; the essential point was that Waverley should be forced by circumstance first to become a Jacobite and then to abandon the failing cause, and should be able to do all this without loss of honor.

Characterization

Scott was not the kind of writer to be interested in technical experiments or in literary form for its own sake. Waverley's point of view is preserved with fair consistency, no doubt because it provides the author an opportunity to describe "manners" at length (everything seen was new to Waverley). Other characters reveal themselves primarily by speech and action, but Scott does not hesitate to offer an occasional interior view, especially to make us better acquainted with a major character at his first introduction. Like Fielding, the author comments freely, in his own person, and at least a few readers objected to these violations of realism. Even the enthusiastic Miss Edgeworth complained: "We were so possessed with the belief that the whole story and every character in it was real, that we could not endure the occasional addresses from the author to the reader."[12] But such arguments had no weight for

Scott. To him, as to Johnson, the reader was perfectly aware of the illusion at every moment.

A common judgment of Scott's contemporaries was that his characters were better than his plots, and the success of the work depended in large part on its characters—although certainly not on those of the official hero and heroine, Waverley and Rose Bradwardine. The passionate and tragic Flora Mac-Ivor strongly attracted sentimental readers, who felt that Waverley should have married her. (Scott's comment was that Flora would have set him up on the mantel as the wife of "Count Boralski," a Polish dwarf, was said to have done with her husband.) But Flora is very much a stage heroine and her language is often the language of melodrama: "There is, Mr. Waverley, there is, a busy devil at my heart, that whispers—but it were madness to listen to it—that the strength of mind on which Flora prided herself has murdered her brother . . . it haunts me like a phantom; I know it is unsubstantial and vain; but it *will* be present; will intrude its horrors on my mind." Flora's early appearance, complete with an assortment of picturesque clichés—harp, "shaggy corpse," and "romantic waterfall"—to sing a Highland war song to Waverley, produces an effect of artificiality from which her characterization never recovers.

It is conceivable that the effect is intended, offering an ironic judgment on Flora as at least an occasional poseur, but such an interpretation seems inconsistent with her character and with the tone in which she is presented. Unlike her brother, who expects an earldom for his services, Flora is selfless in her devotion to the Jacobite cause. If Fergus embodies "aggression and desire in action," as one recent critic observes, then Flora symbolizes "desire idealized, divorced from the contamination of intrigue and practicality."[13] Brother and sister alike hope to annex Waverley for their cause, while he in turn desires to gain their passionate energy for himself. Both sides fail.

Fergus won the sympathy of readers away from the official hero almost as effectively as Flora did from the heroine. He is the opposite of Waverley. Waverley is rich, Fergus poor; Waverley is passive, Fergus incessantly active; Waverley submits to circumstance or to the stronger personality, Fergus dominates; Waverley is blond, Fergus dark. He is the energetic "dark hero" that Scott often opposes to the passive, "official" hero. If all the conventional virtue is with the passive hero, all the life is with the dark hero. Even his language often has a colloquial ease and vigor that contrast strikingly with the official hero's pompous diction. Significantly, the dark hero always dies; Scott seems to have admired his qualities yet feared their consequences for society. The narrative poems had already made the pattern familiar. One reader recognized *Waverley* as Scott's work by, among other clues, "the hanging of the clever hero and the marrying of the stupid one."

But Fergus is not merely a typical "dark hero." He is an individual of "bold, ambitious, and ardent, yet artful and politic character," firmly placed in his unique cultural and historical setting. A Highland chief of Jacobite sympathies in the year 1745, he is an incongruous mixture of impulse and calculation, of pride and dissimulation, of Highland barbarism and Gallic sophistication. A chapter of analysis presents Fergus's history and reveals how thoroughly he is the creature of his time and position: "Had Fergus lived Sixty Years sooner than he did, he would, in all probability, have wanted the polished manner and knowledge of the world which he now possessed; and had he lived Sixty Years later, his ambition and love of rule would have lacked the fuel which his situation now afforded." Here the author's commentary is thoroughly justified; it increases the reader's understanding of Fergus and provides the necessary information in the most efficient and economical manner. The chapter is a little historical essay, illuminating in itself and also essential to the novel.

The most complex of the major characters is Baron Bradwardine, in part a military pedant modeled on Shakespeare's Fluellen, in Shakespeare's *Henry V*, but considerably more complex. Like Fergus, he is introduced by a brief sketch of his background and a summary of his character, in which "the pedantry of the lawyer" is superimposed upon "the military pride of the soldier." (The Baron has had a legal education, and later served in the French armies.) He is then allowed to reveal himself in his welcome to Waverley as a litigious, impoverished, rank-conscious gentleman who is proud of his Latin tags and French phrases. His pride is enormous yet inoffensive, perhaps because so naively unconscious—as demonstrated in his comment on the Laird of Killancureit, whose father had been a steward: "And God forbid, Captain Waverley, that we of irreproachable lineage should exult over him, when it may be, that in the eighth, ninth, or tenth generation, his progeny may rank in a manner, with the old gentry of the country." The irony of this mock humility is excellent in itself and still more so in its innocent self-revelation.

In his intense consciousness of rank and family, his despotic authority over his tenants, and his devoted Jacobitism, the Baron closely resembles Fergus Mac-Ivor, but Scott carefully discriminates between the two characters. The baron's power, limited to one wretched village, seems a ridiculous anachronism. He is absurd in success (as in his insistence on his hereditary privilege of removing the boots of his sovereign after a battle), but heroic in defeat. His culture is solidly founded on classical literature, and his allusions remind us of a broader world than Scotland and of the essential continuity of the human condition. He is a pedant, yet capable of translating the Latin poets into vigorous Scots. The character is much more than a mere "humour," as similar figures often became in Scott's later works.

Scott's own favorite character, though he did not expect his choice to be anyone else's, was Bailie MacWheeble, manager of the Baron's estate. Cautious (if not cowardly), selfish, calculating, sly, and self-serving, yet devoted to his master's interests (next to his own), he is a type that Scott loved to portray. The Bailie's combination of subservience toward superiors and of arrogance toward inferiors is revealed even in his position at the table:

to preserve that proper declination of person which showed a sense that he was in the presence of his patron, he sat upon the edge of his chair, placed at three feet distance from the table . . . projecting his person towards it in a line which obliqued from the bottom of his spine . . . . This stooping position might have been inconvenient to another person; but long habit made it, whether seated or walking, perfectly easy to the worthy Bailie. In the latter posture, it occasioned, no doubt, an unseemly projection of the person towards those who happened to walk behind, but those being at all times his inferiors . . . he cared very little what inference of contempt or slight regard they might derive from the circumstance.[14]

Language

Whenever a lower-class character appears, speaking either his native Scots or a lofty biblical English—for this is a Bible-saturated culture—that person comes instantly and memorably to life, no matter how brief his or her appearance. A blacksmith's wife of Jacobite sympathies, a "strong, large-boned, hard-featured woman, about forty, dressed as if her clothes had been flung on with a pitchfork," scornfully addresses the people of her village: "And that's a' your Whiggery, and your presbytery, ye cut-lugged, graining carles! What! d'ye think the lads wi' the kilts will care for yer synods and yer presbyteries, and yer buttock-mail, and yer stool o' repentance?"

Equally expressive is the plea of the village elders: "Whisht, gudewife; is this a time; or is this a day, to be singing your ranting fule sangs in?—a time when the wine of wrath is poured out without mixture in the cup of indignation, and a day when the land should give testimony against popery, and prelacy, and quakerism, and independency, and supremacy, and erastianism, and antinomianism, and a' the errors of the church?" Presbyterian fanatic, village shrew, or drunken horse trader, Scott presents them objectively; and he allows them, unlike his aristocrats, to speak their native dialect. (Given her time and place, Rose Bradwardine would have spoken Scots, but her language is as formal and "correct" as Waverley's. In the Waverley novels a heroine, like a hero, *must* speak standard English, whatever historical accuracy might demand.) By literary convention a hero is a gentleman, a heroine is a lady—and their social status must be established by the "correctness" of their speech, which instantly distinguishes them from the lower-class characters by whom they are surrounded. These characters, in turn, promptly recognize the gentleman by his speech, whatever his outward circumstance may be, and treat him with a proper respect.

Primarily, the effectiveness of characterization in *Waverley* depends upon the language that the characters speak; the more strongly Scottish the speech, the more vigorous and individual the character. At one extreme are the peasants and burghers speaking their broad Scots; at the other are the hero and heroine, conversing in standard English. But to call it "standard English" is misleading; no language resembling it could ever have been spoken. It is trite, redundant, Latinate, involved; often absurd, it is disastrous when intense feeling is to be expressed. Out of a hundred possible examples, one may consider the dialogue in which Flora rejects Waverley's suit, and he asks her reasons:

"Forgive me, Mr. Waverley," said Flora . . . . "I should incur my own heavy censure, did I delay expressing my sincere conviction that I can never regard you otherwise than as a valued friend . . . oh, better a thousand times, Mr. Waverley, that you should feel a present momentary disappointment, than the long and heart-sickening griefs which attend an ill-assorted marriage!"

"Good God!" exclaimed Waverley, "why should you anticipate such consequences from a union, where birth is equal, where fortune is favourable, where, if I may venture to say so, the tastes are similar, where you allege no preference for another, where you even express a favourable opinion of him whom you reject?"

Hardly the language of passion! One notes the hackneyed remark that Waverley can only be a friend; the elaborate parallelism of Waverley's reply—"where birth," "where fortune," "where the tastes," "where you allege," "where you even"—carried on through five subordinate clauses; the redundancy of Flora—"*heavy* censure," "*sincere* conviction," "present *momentary* disappointment," "*rash* and ill-assorted marriage"; the careful inversion of "did I delay" and the literally unspeakable "of him whom you reject"; and the absurd propriety of Waverley's "If I may venture to say so." The speaker's surprise and bitter disappointment are simply not communicated. We have Scott's word that Waverley feels strongly; but the author's word is not enough—and here it is directly contradicted by the language of the hero. Strong personal feeling cannot be expressed in such a language.

Colonel Talbot is described as a blunt, practical soldier—common sense incarnate—but this is how he talks in a moment of emotion: "It is a responsibility, Heaven knows, sufficiently heavy for mortality, that we must answer for the foreseen and direct result of our actions,—for their indirect and consequential operation, the great and good Being, who alone can foresee the dependence of human events on each other, hath not pronounced his frail creatures liable." Again, the character's speech destroys the intended impression.

When Scott fails in direct description, again the fault is usually one of language. A description of Fergus Mac-Ivor in a rage: "The veins of his forehead swelled when in such agitation; his nostril became dilated; his cheek and eye inflamed; and his look became that of a demoniac. These appearances of half-suppressed rage were the more frightful because they were obviously caused by a strong effort to temper with discretion an almost ungovernable paroxysm of passion, which agitated his whole frame of mortality." In the first sentence one notices the triteness of the symptoms and their melodramatic exaggeration; in the second, the abstractness of the language and its extreme redundancy—"whole frame of mortality" for "body"—dampening any excitement aroused by the preceding sentence.

Vagueness of language can be both a cause and a consequence of vagueness of conception: "Rose Bradwardine rose gradually in Waverley's opinion. He had several opportunities of remarking that, as her extreme timidity wore off, her manners assumed a higher character; that the agitating circumstances of the stormy time seemed to call forth a certain dignity of feeling and expression that he had not formerly observed; and that she omitted no opportunity within her reach to extend her knowledge and refine her taste." But those phrases about Rose's extending her knowledge and refining her taste, what precisely do they mean? Did she study geometry, perhaps? Or practice the harpsichord?" And generalities such as "dignity of feeling and expression" and the "higher character" of Rose's manners are useless unless realized in action or speech.

Scott fails conspicuously when he attempts to make his hero more interesting and "romantic." At the ball held by the Jacobites at Holyrood Castle in Edinburgh, before the battle of Preston-pans, "Waverley exerted his powers of fancy, animation and eloquence, and attracted the general admiration of the company . . . . Waverley, as we have elsewhere observed, possessed at times a wonderful flow of rhetoric; and . . . touched more than once the higher notes of feeling, and then again ran off in a wild voluntary of fanciful mirth." Finally, the Prince observes that "He is really one of the most fascinating young men whom I have ever seen." But Waverley never *shows* these powers with which he is suddenly credited, and the reader cannot guess what that wonderful flow of rhetoric or that "wild voluntary of fanciful mirth" might have been like. At the end of the scene we are told that Flora has changed her opinion that Waverley's manners indicated "timidity and imbecility of disposition." But the reader is given no reason to change such a judgment.

Passages like these almost justify Edwin Muir's observation that Scott's prose is "a unique combination of bookishness and slovenliness . . . no matter what he has to say, Scott seems resolved to say it in the dullest way possible, and in the slowest."[15] This debased Johnsonese is the principal medium of Scott's narrative. It is objectionable not simply because it is undistinguished, but because it impedes the movement of the story, blurs and generalizes the scenes and actions described, sometimes contradicts the intended effect, and makes impossible the expression of genuine feeling.

Dramatic Presentation

Although Scott never seems to have realized as clearly as his contemporary, Jane Austen, the importance of the dramatic scene for revealing character in action and in interaction, he can at times create an effective and revealing scene. Perhaps the most moving passage in *Waverley* is the trial and condemnation of Fergus Mac-Ivor and his henchman, Evan Dhu. Scott's narrative is clear and concise; his language, understated. Fergus's dignified speech of defiance to the judge is immediately offset by the simplicity and unconscious humor of Evan's appeal for the life of his chief: "let him gae back to France, and no to trouble King George's government again, that ony six o' the very best of his clan will be willing to be justified in his stead; and if you'll just let me gae down to Glennaquoich, I'll fetch them up to ye mysell, to head or hang, and you may begin wi' me . . . ." Scott splits the Highland character, one critic has noted, with Evan representing its potentiality for fidelity and self-sacrifice while Callum Beg, Fergus's murderous young body-servant, embodies its "latent anarchy and destructiveness." The moving simplicity of Evan's reproof to the laughing audience follows: "If they laugh because they think I would not keep my word, and come back to redeem him, I can tell them they ken neither the heart of a Hielandman, nor the honor of a gentleman." Evan speaks in the vernacular; Scott never achieves such a quality with standard English.

An even more striking effect is obtained, again with the vernacular, when the reader's emotions have been worked upon to the highest degree by

Waverley's final conversation with Fergus in his cell, and by anticipation of the savage punishment (he is to be hanged, drawn, and quartered) that is imminent. As Waverley leaves Carlisle, his servant sums up the matter: "It's a great pity of Evan Dhu, who was a very weel-meaning, good-natured man, to be a Hielandman; and indeed so was the Laird of Glennaquoich too, for that matter, when he wasna in ane o' his tirrivies." Suddenly Scott has brought the reader down from the tragic plane to a level on which he can be expected to take an interest in the winding up of the plot and Waverley's marriage to Rose Bradwardine.

Equally successful is the drinking bout with which Baron Bradwardine welcomes Waverley. The Baron and his cronies, particularly the oafish Balmawhapple, reveal themselves in their natural speech. The increasing befuddlement, as first the Blessed Bear of Bradwardine (the Baron's huge ceremonial goblet) and then the Tappit Hen (the village landlady's pot) circulate, is shown by the growing confusion, the mutual interruptions, the insults and anger that culminate in the inevitable brawl as Bradwardine and Balmawhapple draw their swords on each other. The whole scene is a first-rate piece of comedy, and a brilliant satirical presentation of Scottish "manners." A few chapters later, the description of Fergus's feast for his clan—a scene presenting a society that seems closer to ancient Greece than to eighteenth-century England—offers a companion piece.

Realism and Romance

Scott's contemporaries were usually content to delight in the exciting action, the striking characters, the picturesque scenery, and the faithful accounts of "manners" they found in his novels, without looking for further significance. But it is easily possible to see in *Waverley* a unifying theme, even if not a wholly unified structure. It can be described as a conflict between romance and reality, or in terms of the conflict between Waverley's sound and unsound judgment.

Waverley's early reading disgusts him with the actual world of busy, peaceful, prosperous England, and in Scotland he seems to discover the past of his imagination, of violence, heroism, and adventure. On hearing of a raid on the Baron's cattle by Highland robbers, and Rose's account of past troubles of the same kind, "Waverley could not help starting at a story which bore so much resemblance to one of his own day-dreams. Here was a girl . . . who had witnessed with her own eyes such a scene as he had used to conjure up in his imagination, as only occurring in ancient times. He might have said to himself . . . 'I am actually in the land of military and romantic adventures, and it only remains to be seen what will be my own share in them.'" Traveling toward the cave of the robber Donald Bean Lean, Waverley intensely enjoys himself: "Here he sat on the banks of an unknown lake, under the guidance of a wild native, whose language was unknown to him, on a visit to the den of some renowned outlaw, a second Robin Hood, perhaps . . . . What a variety of incidents for the exercise of his romantic imagination . . . . The only circumstance which assorted ill with the rest, was the cause of his journey—the Baron's milk cows! this degrading incident he kept in the background."

The robber's cave is so intensely picturesque that Waverley "prepared himself to meet a stern, gigantic, ferocious figure, such as Salvator would have chosen to be the central object of a group of banditti." Disillusionment soon follows, when Donald Bean Lean turns out to be "diminutive and insignificant" and is dressed in a cast-off uniform; but Waverley fails to profit by the lesson and to realize that there is nothing in the least romantic about Donald or his exploits. Naturally, Waverley is carried away with enthusiasm when he takes part in the feast of the clan of Ivor. If Tully-Veolan and Baron Bradwardine had seemed almost to return him to feudal times, this tribal society, with the warriors banqueting in their chieftain's hall, seems to belong to a still earlier age.

Waverley, the outsider, is swept away by the romance of the occasion, but Fergus, the chief, is immune—during the bard's song, "The Chieftain . . . had appeared rather to watch the emotions which were excited, than to partake of their high tone of enthusiasm." Waverley's enthusiasm for the Highlanders is merely a superficial pleasure in their picturesque costumes and customs. Its quality is suggested by the "large and spirited painting," which he orders when his adventures are ended, "representing Fergus Mac-Ivor and Waverley in their Highland dress, the scene a wild, rocky, and mountainous pass, down which the clan were descending in the background."

Waverley, then, is prepared for such a "military and romantic adventure" as the Jacobite rising; and any remaining judgment is overcome by the glamour of Prince Charles, who seems to him a "hero of romance." He quickly forgets his commonsense view, that whatever the legal claim of the Stuarts to the throne might be, it was hardly worthwhile "to disturb a government so long settled and established, and to plunge a kingdom into all the miseries of civil war, for the purpose of replacing upon the throne the descendants of a monarch by whom it had been wilfully forfeited." Disenchantment begins almost at once, when Waverley witnesses the reality of civil war at Preston-pans, and it is increased by the arguments of his prisoner, Colonel Talbot, who is entirely immune to the claims of sentiment and romance, and by the total absence of popular enthusiasm as the rebels march into England.

Waverley soon has enough of the glory of war: "The plumed troops and the big war used to enchant me in poetry; but the night marches, vigils, couches under the wintry sky, and such accompaniments of the glorious trade, are not at all to my taste in practice." Adventure, danger, heroism, sacrifice—Waverley learns that these are not merely words in books, but realities that he prefers not to experience. Cut off from the prince's army during a skirmish, and without hope of rejoining it, he "felt himself entitled to say firmly, though perhaps with a sigh, that the romance of his life was ended, and that its real history had now commenced." More accurately, he has withdrawn from history, lucky in being able to do so, as Fergus cannot.

To Waverley at the outset, England represented calculation, restraint, "reality"; Scotland, adventure and "romance," an impulsive yielding to desire. This contrast is repeated in a series of oppositions: Lowland-Highland, Hanoverian-Jacobite, Rose Bradwardine and Flora Mac-Ivor, Colonel Talbot and Fergus, in reality a shrewd and ambitious politician staking his life for an earldom, but to Waverley "the incarnation of romance." By the conclusion of the novel he is quite content to marry Rose, who will make a much more comfortable wife than Flora, and to live a quiet life on his estate. The romance of life is dismissed, "perhaps with a sigh," but nevertheless firmly. Waverley will lead the safe and undemanding life of an affluent and cultivated country gentleman, while carefully preserving his weapons and his Highland dress as souvenirs of his adventurous youth.

This contrast between "romance" and "reality" is carried through the work with a good deal of consistency, yet it seems less important in the total effect than it should be. The reader is not interested enough in Waverley himself, who embodies and illustrates the contrast. His conversion from romance to reality requires a psychological change that Scott does not, probably could not, represent; he simply states from time to time that a change is taking place, and at last that it is concluded. Scott may assure his readers that Waverley finally "acquired a more complete mastery of a spirit tamed by adversity than his former experience had given him"; but the assertion does not convince because it is not demonstrated. The "happy ending" is not made possible by any change in the hero, but by his lucky inheritance of a fortune when his father dies and by the influence of his friends.

What the reader sees is not a hero gradually maturing through the lessons of experience but rather, in the words of a contemporary reviewer, a character "ineffectually repenting, snatched away by accident from his sinking party: by accident preserved from justice; and restored by the exertions of his friends to safety, fortune, and happiness." Waverley is a natural spectator whose simple motivation and psychology allow him to change sides easily and to function as a sort of "historical tourist."

Waverley as a Historical Novel

Waverley must still be considered as a historical novel. The remark of George Lukács, a Marxist critic, that Scott was the first novelist to reveal the "derivation of the individuality of characters from the historical peculiarities of their age"[16] appears justified. (Scott's work has appealed to Marxists for just this reason.) As has been noted, Fergus is carefully placed in his historical moment, and this placement is as effective, although less explicit, for Bradwardine, Colonel Talbot, Evan Dhu Maccombich, Donald Bean Lean, and even Bailie MacWheeble. The historical setting, solid and accurate, is delineated without pedantry or excessive detail.

Scott had read the available sources, but his most important knowledge had been gained firsthand from survivors of the rebellion. His own ancestors had fought for the Stuarts in 1690 and 1715; as a child he had listened to the stories of survivors of the uprising of 1745 and had become "a valiant Jacobite at the age of ten."[17] These events were not part of a remote and alien past; they formed a central part of the recent history of his country. His relationship to them is similar to that of Tolstoy to the Napoleonic invasion of Russia, also some sixty years later. It seems possible that "sixty years since" approaches the limit to which a writer's imagination can penetrate; a novel dealing with the more distant past tends to become an archaeological reconstruction, tempered by anachronisms.

Two other well-known nineteenth-century novels dealing in part with the Jacobite movement, William Makepeace Thackeray's *Henry Esmond* (1852), and Robert Louis Stevenson's *Kidnapped* (1886), provide useful comparisons with *Waverley*. Much of *Kidnapped* is set in the Highlands in the aftermath of the uprising of 1745, while the concluding chapters of *Esmond* deal with efforts to place the Jacobite candidate on the throne after the death of Queen Anne in 1714. Both are written by conscious stylists. Stevenson harshly condemned the slovenliness of Scott's prose, and his own language is concrete, economical, idiomatic—superior in almost every respect. Unlike Scott, he had completely mastered the technique of presenting violent physical action and is unsurpassed in the creation of atmosphere and suspense—for example, David Balfour's climb through darkness and storm up a broken stairway in a ruined tower in his uncle's house. Yet *Kidnapped*, in comparison to *Waverley*, seems almost a "boy's book." History provides a pretext for adventure.

Thackeray at first appears more seriously concerned with historical accuracy than does Scott, even attempting to write an early eighteenth-century prose appropriate to Esmond, his narrator. Yet for all its careful period atmosphere, the work is fundamentally unhistorical and intensely Victorian in the morality and psychology of the continuously judgmental and highly self-conscious Esmond. And Esmond's problem—the conflict between his passion for the lovely Beatrix Castlewood and his almost incestuous devotion to her mother, who has been his foster mother—has no necessary relation to its period.

In dealing with the Jacobite failure, Thackeray's method is radically different from Scott's. As Esmond narrates the complex intrigues surrounding the death of Queen Anne (intrigues that he himself directs), it appears that James, the "Old Pretender," could easily have made himself king if only he had not thrown his chances away through his own weakness and immorality—making love to Beatrix instead of watching events. (Unlike Scott, Thackeray makes his Pretender a major character.) Outraged, Esmond withdraws from the conspiracy, which promptly collapses. History is personified and trivialized. *Waverley*, in contrast, is deeply historical, dramatizing the contrast between Jacobite and Whig, demonstrating the necessity of the Jacobite failure (the Prince himself is a minor figure, appearing briefly in a single chapter), communicating a powerful sense of individuals trying to serve their private ends while caught up a conflict they cannot fully understand and whose outcome and consequences they cannot foresee.

The reader's emotions, like Waverley's, inevitably go with the Jacobites, even though common sense may reluctantly prefer George II to Bonnie Prince Charlie. Certainly Scott's treatment does justice, perhaps a little more than justice, to the rising as a chivalrous adventure. Yet intelligence does not abdicate; it is present in the arguments of Colonel Talbot, and in Waverley's second thoughts as he sees the reality of civil war. An anachronism in the comfortable, rational Great Britain of 1745, the rising is an effort to restore the past, one of "romance" and "honor" perhaps, but also of poverty (strongly emphasized in Scott's description of the village of Tully-Veolan), bloodshed, and disorder. The point is made explicit by Evan Dhu, Fergus's second in command, when he taunts Bailie MacWheeble: "The guid auld times of rugging and riving [pulling and tearing] are come back again" and the law must give way to the longest sword. It is significant, incidentally, that Gifted Gilfillan and his troop of Whiggish irregulars, who seem a reincarnation of the Roundheads and Covenanters of the previous century, are ignominiously routed by the Highlanders. The rebellion is not to be defeated by another anachronism.

One may learn a great deal of history from *Waverley*, in spite of modern and postmodern literary theorists who insist that literature can make only pseudostatements or that texts can refer to nothing outside themselves. Yet it is absurd to insist, as the *Quarterly Review* did, that the interest and value of the work derive "not from any of the ordinary qualities of a novel, but from the truth of its facts, and the accuracy of its delineations."[18] Without the "ordinary [or perhaps extraordinary] qualities" of a novel, *Waverley* would be valueless.

Scott does not give, and clearly did not intend to give, a full picture of the rising. The novel omits the most romantic episodes, notably, the landing of the prince in the Highlands, accompanied by only seven followers, and his adventurous escape after the final defeat at Culloden—both essential to a complete account. Scott was not writing a history but a novel, and his subject was not only the rebellion itself but the ways of feeling and behaving that it allowed him to present—particularly the contrast between a past of passion and violence, represented by Scotland (especially the Highlands) and the Jacobites, and a present of reason and law and prudent self-interest, represented by England and the Hanoverians.

In spite of the glamour of the past, which Scott fully realizes and presents, its defeat is shown to be beneficial, or at any rate necessary. Yet the pathos of its defeat and disappearance is inescapable (the reader should be aware of the destruction of lowland feudalism and Highland clanship and the depopulation of the Highlands that followed the rebellion). There is a sorrow for what is lost, a sense of lessening. We find in *Waverley* a conflict and theme that recurs often in Scott's work, and that provide the underlying unity and seriousness that make *Waverley* a frequently moving and impressive work in spite of its faults of construction and style.

But for the imagination at least, the past has not entirely disappeared—it is present in the pages of this book. Paradoxically, "What Edward Waverley must dismiss, *Waverley* preserves."[19]

Redgauntlet

Ten years after the publication of Waverley, Scott presented in *Redgauntlet* the concluding phase of the Jacobite movement. During the twenty years after 1745, Jacobitism had entered its final decline: it was soon no more than a sentimental or antiquarian affectation, a drinking of toasts to the king across the water, no more significant than displays of the Confederate flag in twentieth-century America. The Highlands had been reduced to order for the first time in history, Scotland had prospered as it never had before, and had begun to produce a brilliant intellectual life. Under such conditions, Jacobitism must have appeared simply irrelevant. Nevertheless, hope died slowly among the faithful, and historians record a succession of plots, always unsuccessful and usually betrayed to the government. One of these even brought Charles Edward, the Pretender, to London. Hugh Redgauntlet's plot, and the accompanying return of Charles, are fictional, but could easily have been fact.

No other Scott novel is dominated so completely by a single character. If the book contrasts the old Scotland and the new, the old is summed up in Redgauntlet, a man who not only dreams the past but lives it. His first appearance is revealing; he is engaged in salmon-spearing from horseback and, of course, his skill surpasses everyone else's. The sport—picturesque, adventurous, and archaic—is typical of the man; and the contrast of old ways and new is symbolized by the contrast between Redgauntlet's fish-spearing and the vastly more efficient fish traps of the Quaker Joshua Geddes. Redgauntlet's dress is symbolic of the man himself and of his cause; it "was not in the present taste, and though it had once been magnificent, was not antiquated and unfashionable." His physical strength and his skill in sports and with weapons are great, and his personal force is such that he intimidates everyone he meets. His determination, energy, and intelligence have enabled him single-handedly to hold the Jacobite movement together, and to persuade its reluctant leaders to act, or at any rate promise to act, once more. Like Melville's Ahab, Redgauntlet bends all his formidable energies to a monomaniacal pursuit of an unattainable goal, overawing all those with whom he comes in contact and compelling their support.

But his weaknesses are as obvious as his strength. Violence always seems possible when he is present, for his temper is savage and scarcely under control. A more serious weakness still is his inability to recognize, or admit, unwelcome reality. He simply refuses to acknowledge the political and social changes that have taken place during twenty years. He kidnaps his nephew, Darsie, because of Darsie's supposed authority over the tenants of the former Redgauntlet estates (which were confiscated after the uprising of 1745). But the effort is useless; even if Darsie gave the order to rise in rebellion (which he has no intention of doing),no one would follow him because the feudal allegiance of tenant to landlord has been annulled. A conversation between Darsie and his sister Lilias reveals the reality:

"Whatever these people may pretend to evade your uncle's importunities, they cannot, at this time of day, think of subjecting their necks again to the feudal yoke,

which was effectually broken by the Act of 1748, abolishing vassalage and hereditary jurisdiction."

"Ay, but that my uncle considers as the act of a usurping government," said Lilias.

"Like enough *he* may think so," answered her brother, "for he is a superior, and
loses his authority by the enactment. But the question is what the vassals will think of
it, who have gained their freedom from feudal slavery, and have now enjoyed that
freedom for many years?"

Throughout the novel there is this sense of a changing time. Much of the
action takes place by the Solway River, on the border between Scotland and
England, and John Buchan has commented justly that "in the book we have
the sense of being always on a borderland—not only between two different
races, but between comfort and savagery and between an old era and a new."
(That statement also applies to *Old Mortality, The Bride of Lammermoor*, and
Ivanhoe—even to *Guy Mannering* and *The Antiquary*, although less obviously and less dramatically.) In this new era, Redgauntlet's qualities are no
longer the most valuable. Old Saunders Fairford, lawyer and good Whig,
may have fled rather ingloriously at the Battle of Falkirk during the rebellion,
but his son defends him: "He has courage enough to do what is right, and to
spurn what is wrong—courage enough to defend a righteous cause with
hand and purse, and to take the part of the poor man against his oppressor,
without fear of the consequences to himself. This is civil courage . . . and it is
of little consequence to most men in this age and country whether they ever
possess military courage or no." Courage of this kind is less showy than
Redgauntlet's but more useful to society. Scotland has become a society of
law in which, as old Mr. Fairford puts it, only soldiers and thieftakers need to
bear arms.

The novel of course includes an official hero—two of them, in fact, Darsie
Latimer and his intimate friend, Alan Fairford, a promising young lawyer.
Darsie is a young man with a comfortable income and no occupation, who is
completely ignorant of his own background. (His money is paid to him by a
London banker.) Darsie has no relation to society, he simply draws an income. As he says of himself, he is like "a stranger in a crowded coffee house"
who enters, calls out his order, "pays his bill, and is forgotten as soon as the
waiter's mouth has pronounced his 'thank ye, sir.'" It is the typical position of
the Scott hero, carried to the extreme. The disconnected man's search for his
place in society offers a promising theme, but it is quickly superseded by
Redgauntlet's plotting.

Visiting the remote, half-savage region of the Solway estuary, the boundary between Scotland and England, a region that he vaguely feels is con-

nected with himself, Darsie is saved from drowning by a mysterious stranger, Hugh Redgauntlet. Gradually he learns something of the disastrous past of the Redgauntlets, violent men who seem cursed to fight always on the losing side. It is a history that appears somehow to recapitulate the history of Scotland. Rescued again by Redgauntlet, Darsie is held prisoner by him, falls sick, after his recovery is forced to disguise himself as a woman, and is entirely helpless for the remainder of the novel.

Even more passive than Waverley, Darsie is often absurd (as when he attempts to make love to Redgauntlet's beautiful niece, Lilias, and is deeply shocked when she enthusiastically kisses him, until he discovers that Lilias is his sister and then—himself a prisoner in woman's clothes—dramatically offers her his protection!) Alan at first seems more active. He has met Lilias and fallen in love with her, and a good deal of the narrative deals with his search for Lilias and his friend, but he too is captured by Jacobites, falls sick, and remains a helpless prisoner after his recovery, morally dominated by "Father Buonaventure" (the Pretender in disguise) as Waverley is dominated by his uncle.

As usual in a Scott novel, there are picturesque supporting figures: Tom Trumbull, paymaster of smugglers, a pious hypocrite whose prayer book is illustrated with pornographic drawings; and Wandering Willie, a blind musician who tells Darsie a diabolical legend of the Redgauntlet family. (Told in Scots dialect, Willie's tale is the only occasion in the Waverley Novels when Scott uses the vernacular as a medium for narrative.) But the most notable among the lesser characters is Peter Peebles, a striking grotesque in his ancient wig, shrunken till it perches on the top of his head, where it supports an "immense cocked hat." Like a figure from Dickens, Peebles has been reduced to beggary and near-madness by an endless, infinitely complicated lawsuit.

In fact, Peebles is as pure a fanatic for the law as Redgauntlet is for the cause of the Pretender. He becomes considerably more than comic relief when he remarks of an old woman whom he had once prosecuted for debt: "She might live or die, for what I care . . . . What business have folk to do to live that canna live as the law will, and satisfy their just and lawful creditors?" Peebles and Redgauntlet both devote their lives to their cause and are prepared to sacrifice others; both refuse to acknowledge a hostile reality. Scott enforces the parallel when Peebles exclaims, "A great year it was; the Grand Rebellion broke out, and my cause—the great cause—Peebles against Plainstanes . . . was called in the beginning of the winter session." Such a parallel suggests that Redgauntlet's heroics are not to be taken with complete seriousness.

Redgauntlet's plot is desperate; he plans to raise five hundred men, seize the town of Carlisle (where Fergus Mac-Ivor had been executed), and proclaim Charles king. Then he will wait for the Highland regiments to defect, for disbanded soldiers to join the cause, and for the English Jacobite landlords to raise their people. He exaggerates every appearance of discontent and takes them as signs of readiness for revolution. That the plot is hollow, the reader is never allowed to doubt. "You'll as soon raise the dead as raise the Highlands; you'll as soon get a grunt from a dead sow as any comfort from Wales or Cheshire," remarks the realistic Nanty Ewart, who explains Redgauntlet's apparent success: "He gets encouragement from some, because they want a spell of money from him; and from others, because they fought for the cause once, and are ashamed to go back; and others, because they have nothing to lose; and others, because they are discontented fools."

The final scene, in which the "bubble," as the plot is often referred to, explodes, is the most complex and significant of the novel. It has been thoroughly prepared for, and our curiosity has been most successfully aroused (not through suspense as to what will happen, for we know that the plot must fail, but through curiosity as to how much substance Redgauntlet's conspiracy actually has, and how he will react to failure). (Unlike Ahab, he outlives his defeat.) The Jacobite leaders have gathered, at Redgauntlet's urging, for what they think is merely a consultation but what he considers to be the prelude to instant rebellion.

The meeting itself shows the hopelessness of the cause, in the reluctance of the conspirators and in their growing dismay as Redgauntlet removes one by one their pretexts for delay, until at last they learn that Charles is actually there, ready to lead them. Then Charles defeats his own cause (as his ancestors had so often done) by his stubborn logic. When the conspirators learn that he has brought his mistress, whom they suspect of treachery, with him, they demand, as a condition of their support, that he abandon her. Charles refuses, although he no longer cares for her. Subjects cannot dictate to their king, for the king would be no king under such conditions.

To ensure the defeat of the plotters, who are already divided and about to withdraw, government troops arrive (the whole scheme has been betrayed, not by Charles's mistress but by Redgauntlet's own servant), and the Jacobites suddenly rally and determine at least to die heroically in defense of their prince. A dramatic moment ensues when Charles refuses to flee: "Many threw themselves at his feet with weeping and entreaty; some one or two slunk in confusion from the apartment, and were heard riding off." The entrance at this moment of General Campbell, the government commander, is a triumph of understatement: "Amid this scene of confusion, a gentleman, plainly dressed in a riding-habit, with a black cockade [the Hanoverian emblem] in his hat, but without any arms except a *couteau-de-chasse*, walked into the apartment without ceremony."

Beside the Jacobites, he seems an incarnation of common sense and practicality. Campbell's announcement is surprising but logical: the plotters are asked only to return home quietly and everything will be forgotten, while Charles is free to embark for the Continent. Officially, the general declines to recognize the Pretender's existence. "The cause is lost forever!" exclaims Redgauntlet, and he is right. No one but himself will go with Charles into exile. In a Shakespearean echo that is surely intended, Redgauntlet lays his hand on his sword and promises to "sink it forty fathoms deep in the wide ocean," as Prospero in *The Tempest* had promised to abjure his "rough magic," to break his staff and drown his book of power "deeper than did every plummet sound." In due course, Scott tells us, Redgauntlet forswears the world (again like Prospero) and retires into a monastery where he distinguishes himself by the strictness of his devotions.

So Jacobitism is not allowed a final flourish of heroism and martyrdom; it is simply dismissed as something that no longer matters. Scott's theme, David Daiches has remarked, is the absurdity or irrelevance of heroic action, and the entire novel has presented a world in which there is no place for a Redgauntlet or for the Jacobite cause. From a realistic point of view, Redgauntlet, with "his stately bearing, his fatal frown, his eye of threat and of command," may seem exaggerated and his plans may appear fantastic, but that is precisely the point. Daiches attributes this quality to Scott's conscious design, referring to his "melodramatic posturings (which are not defects in the novel; Scott introduces them deliberately)," and he adds that these posturings "reveal the essential unreality of the world he lives in." The point, however, seems to be not that Redgauntlet is a poseur—he is truly heroic—but that even genuine heroism, in such a cause, cannot help seeming slightly absurd. (And perhaps heroism of this old-fashioned kind, whatever the cause it may be devoted to, is disruptive and troublesome in the modern world.) The theme, Daiches continues, "is a modification of that of Cervantes, and, specifically *Redgauntlet* is Scott's *Don Quixote*."[20] This comment is acceptable if one does not try to press the parallel too far, and if one remembers that Redgauntlet is not the only Quixote in the Waverley Novels.

And the conventional plot must be wound up as well. While Redgauntlet goes into lifelong exile, the future of the two "heroes" must be accounted for. In a deeply ironic conclusion, addressed by "Dr. Dryasdust" to "The Author of Waverley," we are informed that Darsie assumes his true identity as Sir Arthur Darsie Redgauntlet and comes into a rich estate and is even introduced to King George III by General Campbell (for once a Redgauntlet has been found on the winning side), and that a marriage is announced between Miss Lilias Redgauntlet of Redgauntlet and "Alan Fairford, Esq., Advocate, of Clinkdollar." This is the world that has replaced the violent, passionate world of Redgauntlet, who could master everything but history. But this "happy" ending seems curiously ironic and incomplete. Alan's prosperity becomes a crude amassing of dollars, and while Darsie may have gained a name and a title, he still seems an unattached man. Like Waverley, he has lost his illusions, but he has not found Waverley's compensations.

In the conflict between past and present that *Redgauntlet* presents, a past of emotion and violence, a present of reason and moderation, or at least of law—a conflict always involving a sorrow for what is lost, a sense of lessening—we see again a major theme of *Waverley*. It is Scott's most characteristic theme, and nowhere is this pathos deeper than in the conclusion of *Redgauntlet*.

Chapter Five
Guy Mannering and *The Antiquary*

The year 1814 was amazingly productive for Scott, even by his standards. After writing most of *Waverley*, a *Life of Swift*, and *The Lord of the Isles* (another narrative poem, dealing with the career of Robert the Bruch and describing the Battle of Bannockburn), in the final six weeks he tossed off *Guy Mannering*, a three-volume novel. Perhaps he did not entirely trust the success of *Waverley*, or perhaps he was unwilling to give up the form in which he had triumphed. But *The Lord of the Isles* was a failure. Scott responded to the setback like a good businessman, simply remarking that since one line had failed, he must try another.

When *Guy Mannering* appeared in May of 1815 its success was immediate. Scott had become a novelist and remained one for the rest of his career, in spite of many distractions. But it was not "Scott" who became the most-admired writer of his day, throughout Europe and America as well as in Great Britain. His name appeared on no title pages. *Guy Mannering*, and the novels that followed it were attributed simply to "The Author of Waverley"—an identity that soon came to carry a greater significance than any mere personal name could possess. Perhaps more important still, even a nominal anonymity conferred imaginative freedom on the author, allowing him, as one modern critic has observed, "to explore, through the displacements of fiction, some of the inmost concerns of Walter Scott of Abbotsford."[1]

Guy Mannering

The qualities in *Guy Mannering* that delighted Scott's contemporaries are presented by Lockhart in a comprehensive statement: "The easy transparent flow of its style; the . . . wild, solemn magnificence of its sketches of scenery; the rapid . . . interest of the narrative, the unaffected kindliness of feeling, the manly purity of thought, everywhere mingled with a gentle humour and a homely sagacity, but, above all, the rich variety and skillful contrast of characters and manners, at once fresh in fiction, and stamped with the unforgettable seal of truth and nature; these were charms that spoke to every heart and mind."[2]

Lockhart praised the "rapid interest" of the narrative, but carefully makes no mention of its construction—which no critic has ever praised. As Scott confesses in his introduction (composed later) for the "Magnum Opus," the collected edition of his novels, he had, in effect, begun to write one novel, then had decided to write another. He had first intended to base his story on a tale he heard in his childhood about an astrologer whose prediction of great danger for the hero on his twenty-first birthday is fulfilled. He had planned to make his story "out of the incidents of the life of a doomed individual, whose efforts at good and virtuous conduct were to be forever disappointed by the intervention . . . of some malevolent being, and who was at last to come off victorious from the fearful struggle."

The projected scheme may be traced in the three or four first chapters of the work, but further consideration induced the author to lay his purpose aside. But, Scott explains, since he had changed his plans while the novel was "in the course of printing"—he sent his pages of manuscript to the printer as fast as they were written—"the early sheets retained the vestiges of the original tenor of the story, although they now hang upon it as an unnecessary and unnatural encumbrance." So Guy Mannering's astrological forecast remains, although it has no real function and is quite inconsistent with Mannering's character as it is later developed.

In place of his original scheme, Scott developed a story of a missing heir. Harry Bertram, last male descendant of an ancient and decaying family, the Bertrams of Ellangowan, is kidnapped by the smuggler Dirk Hatteraick—fulfilling Mannering's prophecy that his fifth year would be particularly dangerous—and taken to Holland, where he is adopted by a wealthy merchant named Vanbeest. As a young man, ignorant of his identity, he accidentally returns to his native region, under the name of Vanbeest Brown. The Bertram estate has been usurped by the lawyer Glossin, who recognizes young Bertram, or Brown as he is called, and with the aid of Hatteraick, tries to dispose of him. "Brown" survives their machinations and is finally restored to his name, his estate, and his place in society. The novel takes its name from the English Colonel Mannering, who as a young man traveling in the region had cast young Bertram's horoscope, and who as a retired soldier settles in the area and whose daughter Bertram finally marries.

If anything, Guy Mannering showed a regression in technique from Waverley. In it Scott reverts at times to the epistolary technique popularized by Samuel Richardson in his *Pamela* and *Clarissa* seventy years before. It is a device that he often handles awkwardly. Colonel Mannering, on returning to Scotland after seventeen years, immediately sits down to write to a friend in order to tell him everything that has happened during that time. Scott quotes from Sheridan's burlesque, *The Critic*, for the epigraph to one of his chapters, and this letter recalls an earlier passage in that play, when Mr. Puff defends his tragedy against criticism. Sneer has remarked that there is no one reason for one character to be so communicative as to relate to the audience, on his first appearance, all of the background information they need to follow the action. "Egad," answers Puff, "that is one of the most ungrateful observations I ever heard—for the less inducement he has to tell all this, the more I think you ought to be oblig'd to him; for I am sure you'd know nothing of the matter without it." Certainly without that letter we could not know that Mannering had fought a duel with Brown, in India, and believes that Brown had meant to seduce either his wife or his daughter.

Andrew Lang, in his introduction to *Guy Mannering* in the Border Edition of the Waverley Novels, advises us not to analyze but to read, and if we do so, we find obvious attractions. In place of the Highlanders and Jacobites of *Waverley*, there are gypsies and smugglers, a pair of heroes (Charles Hazlewood, son of a neighboring landowner, is in love with Lucy Bertram, against his father's wishes), or three, if Mannering is counted, besides matching heroines and a brace of sharply contrasted villains, the brutish Hatteraick and the calculating Glossin. There is picturesque scenery and country sports, lovingly described. There is high life and there is low life. There are Meg Merrilies, the ancient gypsy sibyl, and Dandie Dinmont, the rough but good-hearted farmer, and Dandie's dogs, the innumerable Peppers and Mustards. The episodes include a jailbreak, an attack by smugglers on a country house, a combat with robbers, a presentation of gypsy burial customs, a kidnapping, and a mysterious murder. There is even a touch of the detective story when Dirk Hatteraick is convicted of murdering the gauger (customs officer) Frank Kennedy seventeen years earlier because his foot matched the measurements taken of footprints at the scene of the crime.

Most of all, Scott's readers enjoyed the characters. Dinmont, Meg, and even Hatteraick were compared, for their originality and truth, to the characters of Shakespeare—a comparison that became standard among Scott's admirers. The most admired was Meg Merrilies, a striking figure with her red cloak and her six-foot height. She seems an embodiment of Fate: "Tell him the time's coming now, and the weird's dreed, and the wheel's turning." But Scott alternately exaggerates the character and treats her with excessive caution. Scott's rationalism did not allow him to present her with complete seriousness; he needed to reassure his enlightened audience that *he* was not taken in by gypsy superstitions.

Yet in Guy Mannering, those who interfere with old ways come to no good. Swollen with self-importance at being made a justice of the peace, Bertram rashly overturns long-established way and brings disaster on himself in doing so. By his authority, the beggar is sent to the workhouse, the idiot to prison, and even the pedlar is forbidden to make his rounds. Worst of all, he evicts a colony of gypsies who had lived for generations on the Ellangowan estate—fishing and hunting, fiddling and piping at merry-makings, telling fortunes, stealing when opportunity offered. Scott, the Tory, might be expected to approve of this energetic smartening up of the lower orders of society, but there is a deeper Toryism. "All this good," as he calls it, "had its rateable proportion of evil. Even an admitted nuisance of ancient standing, should not be abated without some caution."

Like the ideologues of the French Revolution, or the Whigs of the early nineteenth century who with their "reforms" seemed bent on destroying everything that made Scotland Scottish, Bertram has forgotten that society is an organic whole, in which all of its members and all of its customs and institutions are related. What happens to the beggar must affect the gentleman. While the gypsy cabins burn, Meg curses him, darkly prophesying disaster: "Ride your ways, Laird of Ellangowan—ride your ways, Godfrey Bertram! This day ye have quenched seven smoking hearths—see if the fire in your ain parlour burn the blyther for that."

Her prophecy is fulfilled in the ways that cut most deeply: his son and heir is kidnapped and his estate is stolen from him by his cheating agent, Glossin. And Bertram too has his curse to give. Senile and dying, he rouses himself as his estate is put up for auction to denounce Glossin: "Out of my sight, ye viper!—ye frozen viper, that I warmed till ye stung me!—Art thou not afraid that the walls of my father's dwelling should fall and crush thee limb and bone?" And Glossin, like Bertram, is duly crushed.

Less striking than Meg, but more credible, Dandie Dinmont was the favorite of more discriminating readers. Certainly Dinmont is the most complex character of the novels. His forthright energy in action and speech wins immediate sympathy, and new aspects of his character are revealed as the novel progresses, such as the vigorous contempt for hypocrisy he displays at the funeral of the elderly Miss Bertram. As the ostentatiously grieving relatives (who are eagerly waiting for the will to be read) quarrel about who should carry the coffin, Dinmont loudly interrupts: "I think ye might hae at least gi'en me a leg o' her to carry . . . God! and it hadna been for the rigs o' land, I would hae gotten her a' to carry mysell, for as mony gentles as are here."

To the *Edinburgh Review*, in his characterization of Dinmont Scott had created "the best rustic portrait that has ever yet been exhibited . . . the most honourable to rustics . . . the truest to nature, the most complete in all its lineaments."[3] Never in English literature had such a character been presented at such length, or so sympathetically. Inevitably, there is still condescension. *Guy Mannering* never implies that Dinmont, honest as he may be, is in any sense equal to a gentleman. The proper social distance is carefully preserved by the gentleman of the novel and by Dinmont himself. Yet in his presentation of Dandie Dinmont the conservative Scott had taken a long step toward democratizing the English novel, making possible George Eliot's Adam Bede and the novels of Thomas Hardy, works demonstrating that the inner life of a village carpenter (in *Adam Bede*) or a peasant girl (in *Tess of the D'Urbervilles*) might be as complex, as troubled, and as interesting as that of any member of the upper classes.

Of the remaining characters, Dominie Sampson, the bore, is a bore indeed with his incredible absent-mindedness and his endlessly repeated "Pro-digious!" (Scott's bores, pedants, and fools, who strongly resemble each other, are generally constructed around some single "humour" or turn of speech, following a convention of the eighteenth-century novel.) As for the "hero," he arouses some interest as the plebeian Vanbeest Brown, who resents the "aristocratic oppression" of Colonel Mannering, but interest in Bertram-Brown diminishes when his identity as the missing heir is revealed. Following the instructions of Meg Merrilies, who knows the secret of his birth and means to reveal it in her own time and way, he sinks into total passivity—"Bertram, resolving to be passive in the hands of a person who had just rendered him such a distinguished piece of service, got into the chaise as directed." That resolve to be passive continues until the end of the story, from which he disappears during long intervals. "By the knocking Nicholas! he'll plague you, now he's come over the herring-pond," Hatteraick tells Glossin. "When he was so high, he had the spirit of thunder and lightning." But never is Brown-Bertram given speech or action to support that description. It is simply his existence, rather than any act of his, that plagues Glossin.

Guy Mannering, then, appears to be a "fluid pudding," in Henry James's phrase—a heap of adventures, melodrama, sometimes original and sometimes hackneyed characters, heavy English and lively Scots dialogue, plus a good deal of miscellaneous lore about the Scottish countryside. Its weaknesses enable us to see more clearly how *Waverley* owed to its subject, the conflict of Jacobite and Hanoverian (but with implications so much wider), that gave it weight and unity. Although *Guy Mannering* is set in the Scotland of the 1760s, the reader is hardly conscious of "history" at all (there are casual references to the troubles of the government of the day with the American colonies).

Yet as Alexander Welsh has suggested in his *The Hero of the Waverley Novels*, *Guy Mannering* can be seen as an ideological novel, surprising as that term might seem when applied to such a work. The ideology involved is that of property, honor, status, and gentlemanliness—topics inextricably connected with each other. It is primarily status, not power or wealth (though wealth is essential), that the hero of almost every Scott novel eventually receives. As Brown-Bertram and his newly discovered sister, Lucy, look toward "the seat of their ancestors," Lucy exclaims: "God knows, my dear brother, I do not covet in your behalf the extensive power which the owners of these ruins are said to have possessed so long, and sometimes to have used so ill. But, oh, that I might see you in possession of such relics of their fortune as should give you an honorable independence." The hero is successively deprived of his true name and even of his false one, of his military rank, of his money—in short, of all identity. Until his true birth is revealed, there is literally no place for him in the static and highly structured society of the novel.

Welsh hardly exaggerates when he remarks that "most of the characters in *Guy Mannering* are set up by their author as checks and definitions of rank."[4] Thus, "Sir Robert Hazlewood is a born gentleman, but fails the test of true modesty and minimal good sense." (Hazlewood is neighbor; his son functions as second hero, eventually marrying Lucy Bertram.) Lucy, in contrast, triumphantly passes the test by her accomplishments, her modesty, and her patient endurance of misfortune. The hero is of course a gentleman by definition and is instantly recognized as one by Dinmont. But the perfect gentleman of the novel, in appearance, manners, and feelings, is Colonel Mannering. He is of "handsome, tall, thin figure," with "cast of features grave and interesting, and his air somewhat military. Every point of his appearance bespoke the gentleman." Mannering, that is, possesses the air of command. The ideal profession for a gentleman is military service; Brown-Bertram, although ignorant of his birth, instinctively abandons commerce and possible wealth when the opportunity of a military career is offered to him.

In this deeply conservative novel, even the gypsies dearly love a lord, and for all of the lower-class characters the fall of the house of Bertram and the sale of their estate is a catastrophe, even though it in no way affects them directly. But the social hierarchy, for them, is the source of order and stability, and the fate of the great families provides a vicarious romance. The whole countryside takes an intense interest in the restoration of the heir of Ellangowan to his rightful estate.

As might be expected, the attitude of the two villains, Hatteraick and Glossin, contrasts sharply with this devotion to the principle of social hierarchy. When dealing with a person of higher status, Hatteraick is sullen, insolent, or offensively familiar. Either he does not know his place in the hierarchy or he refuses to accept it. Glossin, on the other hand, accepts the hierarchy but wishes to rise above his proper level. But his manner constantly betrays the false gentleman; he lacks the gentleman's sense of honor and his politeness toward those weaker than himself. Instead, Glossin either blusters or cringes. Faced with a true gentleman, such as Colonel Mannering, Glossin is instantly cowed and abjectly retreats—even though in a physical contest he might very well win, being younger and stronger.

Moreover, his society refuses to accept his pretensions. In the world of the novel, not all of Glossin's ill-gotten wealth can buy the status he craves or win him acceptance as one of the gentlemen of his district. "In the world of the novel," that is; in reality, it seems probable that the Glossins often reached their goal. Certainly *Guy Mannering* foreshadows the preoccupation—almost obsession—of so much Victorian fiction with the question of who is and who is not a gentleman, and of what the criteria of gentlemanliness may be. It is not necessary to credit Scott with a deliberate intention of exploring the ideology of status—which would appear highly unlikely—to agree that the novel is almost a "treatise on real and pretended gentlemen."[5]

The Antiquary

After a short period of uncertainty, *The Antiquary* (1816) became as successful as its predecessor—and no wonder, for it seems in many ways a companion piece to *Guy Mannering*. As one reviewer observed, "the Antiquary is the Pleydel of *Guy Mannering* (both are elderly bachelors with a caustic wit) . . . Meg Merrilies is split into two personages called Edie Ochiltree and Elspeth; Sir Arthur Wardour is Sir Robert Hazlewood"[6] (both foolish gentlemen). But any reader at all familiar with Scott's life will recognize many of his interests and something of his personality in Jonathan Oldbuck, the antiquary. The original preface, or advertisement, claimed that "The present work completes a series of fictitious narratives intended to illustrate the manners of Scotland at three different periods," and the claim contains obvious truth. *Waverley* presented the Scotland of 1745, *Guy Mannering*, that of a generation later, while the period of *The Antiquary* is the 1790s.

Indeed, *The Antiquary*, set at a time when its middle-aged readers were already grown men and women, can be considered a historical novel at all only to the extent that it presents folk customs and beliefs that Scott felt had already died by the time of its writing. The background of the French Revolution, with war between England and France and fear of invasion, causes the hero, a stranger, to be looked on with suspicion and provides matter for conversation and authorial comment. But the Revolution affects the action only at the conclusion, with a false alarm that the French are coming. Considering Scott's methods of work and aversion to planning, it seems unlikely that he deliberately composed a historical triptych, but rather that he recognized a unity in what he had done and after thanking the public for its reception of his novels, the author of Waverley took "respectful leave, as one who is not likely again to solicit their [the public's] favour."

The Antiquary repeats the missing-heir motif of Guy Mannering, but before Lovel is revealed to be Geraldin Nevil, lost son of the Earl of Glenallan, Scott provides an abundance of adventure. Lovel saves Sir Arthur Wardour and his daughter Isabella from drowning when they are trapped between the rising tide and a high cliff, and he fights a duel with the antiquary's fiery young nephew, Hector MacIntyre. A ghost appears to Lovel when he sleeps in a supposedly haunted chamber in the house of Jonathan Oldbuck, the antiquary of the title (Scott is characteristically ambiguous, allowing either a supernatural or a rationalistic explanation of Lovel's vision). There is a mysterious funeral, treasure hunts by night in a ruined abbey, and even an alarm of French invasion, with the whole countryside mustering in defense. Scott's complaint that The Antiquary "wants the romance of Waverley and the adventure of Guy Mannering" because "the period did not admit of so much romantic situation" seems unjustified.

The plot of Waverley had been loose, but the plot of The Antiquary is chaotic, as Scott himself admitted. E. M. Forster has given a devastating summary of it in his Aspects of the Novel, to illustrate the difference between "plot" (in which events are related by cause and effect) and "story" (in which one thing simply happens after another). His point is that in The Antiquary no causal sequence can be discovered among the story's miscellaneous happenings; the only principle of construction is continuously to introduce new characters and episodes that keep the reader's interest alive. Irrelevancies, loose ends, and false scents are many, but Scott can count on his reader's overlooking or forgetting them, out of absent-mindedness or curiosity to see what happens next.

And this primitive satisfaction, says Forster, is all that The Antiquary offers. The desire to know what happens next keeps the reader turning the pages until the story is concluded with the unmasking and punishment of Dousterswivel, the comic villain, and the rescue of his dupe, Sir Arthur Wardour, with the meeting of father and son, and the clearing away of all difficulties that prevent the union of the hero and heroine. The questions raised in the novel are of the kind that, once answered, completely cease to interest the intelligent reader, who will not be much concerned a second time with the problem of how the treasure came to be hidden in the Abbey, or with the mystery of Lovel's identity.

More than in any other of the Waverley novels, the love story here seems an empty convention, as though Scott could not conceive of a novel without a pair of young lovers. The hero and heroine are, if possible, even less individualized than in *Guy Mannering*. Real passion between them has never been hinted at, and no reader can take any deep interest in such sketchy characters. Lovel is introduced in the opening pages as "a young man of genteel appearance," and that phrase sums him up. The heroine, Isabella Wardour, is as ladylike as Lovel is genteel and possesses a "tall and elegant figure." Halfway through the book, the hero disappears for two hundred pages (another parallel to *Guy Mannering*), reappearing at the conclusion to be united with the heroine and his newly discovered father. His absence is hardly noticed.

The English dialogue is as stilted as before, except in some of Oldbuck's satirical speeches (he was too much of a wit for an antiquary, complained one reviewer), and the narrative prose can be verbose, even irrelevant. "Here, then," Scott writes when Lovel, Isabella, and Sir Arthur Wardour are trapped by the rising tide, "they were to await the slow though sure progress of the raging element, something in the situation of the martyrs of the early church, who, exposed by heathen tyrants to be slain by wild beasts, were compelled for a time to witness the impatience and rage by which the animals were agitated, while awaiting the signal for undoing their grates, and letting them loose upon their victims." Inappropriate and obtrusive, the simile destroys whatever tension has been created. "The rocks are of cardboard . . . the tempest is turned on with one hand while Scott scribbles away about Early Christians with the other," Forster observes; "there is no sincerity, no sense of danger in the whole affair; it is all passionless, perfunctory."[7]

Yet Forster is mistaken when he claims that *all* that *The Antiquary* has to offer is the satisfaction of a crude curiosity. A more justified complaint would be that the author has failed to present an action capable of integrating the varied elements of his work. But unlike Wordsworth or Coleridge, Scott never conceived of the literary work as possessing an organic unity. They wrote for a select audience of highly qualified readers; Scott wrote for a mass audience whose tastes he largely shared, and which asked above all that it should be continuously interested in *something*. And if *The Antiquary* is chaotic, undeniably it offers a fertile chaos.

The book's deepest interest lies not in its adventures, still less in its lovers, but in its fully adult characters—primarily in Jonathan Oldbuck, the elderly antiquary, and in Edie Ochiltree, the old beggar. Any reader at all familiar with Scott's life will find a self-portrait, or even a self-parody, in Oldbuck. Like Scott, he is of bourgeois origin (although he lacks Scott's veneration for long-established rank). Like Scott again, he has been bitterly disappointed in love as a young man, and has never quite recovered from that disappointment —though, unlike Scott, he has withdrawn from active life as a consequence. He shares Scott's own antiquarian interests—in old books, old manuscripts, old traditions, old artifacts, old buildings—shares in them to the point of pedantry; at times a shrewd and witty observer of the life around him, he prefers to spend his life attempting to read the text of the past, but often he ludicrously misreads it.

Edie Ochiltree, the last licensed beggar, *is* the past Oldbuck laboriously searches for. Welcomed wherever he goes, equally familiar with the "gentles" and the commoners of his little world, knowing all the customs and traditions of the countryside, he is the last of his kind. A beggar, he yet has his fixed place, like everyone else except the swindling foreigner, Dousterswivel: "And then what wad a' the country about do for want o' auld Edie Ochiltree, that brings news and country cracks frae ane farmsteading to anither, and gingerbread to the lasses, and helps the lads to mend their fiddles, and the gudewives to clout their pans . . . and has skill o' cow-ills and horse-ills, and kens mair auld sangs and tales than a' the barony besides, and gars ilka body laugh wherever he comes?" Edie is almost obsolete; when he dies, no one will take his place. In the rational future that the novel foresees, the lore that he effortlessly possesses will be lost, or will be only partly recovered by antiquarian labor. But Edie's knowledge is preserved in the pages of *The Antiquary*; the novelist has assumed his role.

Again, the Scots dialogue, with its wit, imagery, pathos, and poetry, might almost be the work of a different writer. "He's but a brunt crust," remarks a woman of Sir Arthur Wardour, who is known to be near bankruptcy. An innkeeper remarks, in all seriousness, of a "ganging plea" concerning the boundary of his backyard, which he had inherited from his father and grandfather: "Oh, it's a beautiful thing to see how lang and how carefully justice is considered in this country!" There is the answer of old Mucklebackit, the fisherman, after the death of his son Steenie, when he explains to Oldbuck why he must repair his boat and go out again the next day: "And what would you have me to do, unless I wanted to see four children starve, because one is drowned? It's weel wi' you gentles, that can sit in the house wi' handkerchers at your een, when ye lose a friend; but the like o' us maun to our work again, if our hearts were beating as hard my hammer."

There are brief but concrete and finely imagined scenes of village life, such as the wake for Steenie Mucklebackit, or neighborhood gossips, gathering at the post office like a chorus of Fates, to examine the mail, guess at its contents (and occasionally steam open a letter), blacken the characters of its recipients, and determine who will get their letters at once and who must wait. Scott knew where his strength lay; in his advertisement, or preface, he remarks that in both *Guy Mannering* and *The Antiquary* he had sought his "principal personages" among the lower class, which is "the last to feel the influence of that general polish" that is steadily making human behavior uniform and uninteresting. In that class, he continues, "I have placed some of the scenes, in which I have endeavoured to illustrate the operation of the higher and more violent passions; both because the lower orders are less restrained by the habit of suppressing their feelings, and because I agree with my friend Wordsworth, that they seldom fail to express them in the strongest and most powerful language." But Scott's comment is misleading; except for Edie Ochiltree and the melodramatic old Elspeth, who reveals the secret of Lovel's birth, lower-class characters are not the "principal personages." Instead, they are peripheral to the central action, often irrelevant to it.

Mucklebackit's answer to Oldbuck implies not only a distinction, but a bitterness between classes that Scott could not allow. The Mucklebackits will be patronized by Lovel, the new Lord Glenallan, and the novel ends with the entire community, almost the entire nation, turning out to resist the common enemy—rich and poor, Highland and Lowland, present and past (the Earl of Glenallen, in true feudal style, leads his own retainers to the expected battle). The Tory ideal seems vindicated by this presentation of an integrated society, differentiated yet unified by consciousness that all are members of a single community and therefore have reason to fight—and to resist the subversive doctrines of the Revolution. Even the pacifist Oldbuck, who ridicules war and the military, calls for his ancestral sword; even old Edie turns out, and when Oldbuck observes that he would not have thought Edie had much to fight for, the answer is inspiring: "*Me* no muckle to fight for, sir?—isna there the country to fight for, and the burnsides that I gang daundering beside, and the hearths of the gudewives that gie me my bit bread, and the bits o'weans that come toddling to play wi' me when I come to a landward town?"

As Oldbuck recognizes, "The country's in little ultimate danger, when the beggar's as ready to fight for his dish as the laird for his land." If that remark seems overly complacent, there is a saving touch of irony. The French are *not* coming and the whole excitement is slightly ridiculous—all the more so because the alarm was caused by Oldbuck himself, when a fire he had lighted was mistaken for a beacon fire giving the alarm.

Before *The Antiquary* can end, Lovel must be introduced to his newly dis-

covered father, and we are told that a month later he will marry Isabella
Wardour. But this hardly matters. In this novel, plot seems pure convention.
The reader must take what pleasure he can from satisfying his curiosity as to
what will happen next, while finding a deeper interest in the character of
Oldbuck and in what Lockhart calls "the humbler and softer scenes, the tran-
script of actual Scottish life."

Chapter Six
Old Mortality

In December 1816—six months after the publication of *The Antiquary*—*Tales of My Landlord*, first series, appeared, including *Old Mortality* and *The Black Dwarf*. Scott had planned to write four short novels, each filling a volume and each set in a different district of Scotland. But, as Lockhart remarks, "his imagination once kindled upon any theme, he could not but pour himself out freely—so that notion was soon abandoned,"[1] and *Old Mortality* grew to the customary three-volume length.

Its predecessor, *The Antiquary*, had come closest to the contemporary scene: *Old Mortality*, with its action covering the period 1679–89, represented Scott's deepest plunge into the past up to that time. When Scott began *Waverley* he had been dealing with events "sixty years since." This difference between *Waverley* and *Old Mortality* is significant: in the earlier novel he had drawn heavily, both for episodes and for his general sense of the period, on the stories he had heard from elderly survivors of the uprising of 1745, but no such sources existed for *Old Mortality*. The author was compelled instead to rely entirely on the knowledge he had gained from historical studies, especially from the pamphlets of the period that he had edited, and from traditions reported to him by others.

To base a novel on such material is difficult and represents a common cause of failure in historical fiction. Often the novel is too sparsely furnished to provide the detailed realism necessary for the illusion of fiction, or at the opposite extreme it may be packed with undigested facts apparently transferred straight from the author's notes. In *Old Mortality*, Scott avoids both extremes; the world he creates is solid and convincing, yet there is seldom any pedantic display of information for its own sake. Scott was confident, says Lockhart, "that the industry with which he had pored over a library of forgotten tracts would enable him to identify himself with the time in which they had birth, as completely as if he had listened with his own ears to the dismal sermons of Peden, ridden with Claverhouse and Dalzell in the rout of Bothwell, and been an advocate at the bar of the Privy Council,"[2] and his confidence was justified.

A Divided Country

Although the subject of *Old Mortality*—the rebellion of the Cameronians, Presbyterian extremists who refused to acknowledge the royal authority—was suggested by chance to Scott, it seems an inevitable choice. It offered an opportunity for the kind of dramatic contrast of strikingly different cultures that he had successfully exploited in *Waverley* but that had not been possible in *Guy Mannering* or *The Antiquary*. Here, the contrast was not between Highlanders but between Cameronians and Royalists, opposed factions of the same society, but the differences were almost as dramatic. "There are noble subjects for narrative during that period," Scott commented, "full of the strongest light and shadow, all human passions stirr'd up and stimulated by the most powerful motives and the contending parties as distinctly contrasted in manners and in modes of thinking as in political principles."[3]

The opening chapter, although marred by the facetiousness of the fictitious Jedediah Cleishbotham (the landlord of *Tales of My Landlord*), establishes the somber tone of the novel and indicates the balance the narrator hopes to achieve in writing of long-dead controversies: "If recollection of former injuries, extra-loyalty, and contempt and hatred of their adversaries produced rigour and tyranny in one party, it will hardly be denied, on the other hand, that, if the zeal for God's house did not eat up the conventiclers, it devoured at least . . . no small portion of their loyalty, sober sense, and good breeding." The figure of Old Mortality, an actual historical personage who in a peaceful age devoted his life to preserving the memory of the "killing times" by cleansing the carved epitaphs of the Presbyterian martyrs, suggests the accomplishment of the novel: to revive the memory of those times more effectually than Old Mortality ever could. The sources from which the narrator claims to have gathered his information—traditions reported by small farmers, pedlars, country weavers, tailors—indicate the popular nature of the Presbyterian cause.

The two following chapters, devoted to the *wappenschaw* (literally "weaponshow") or gathering of militia with the accompanying sports and military exercises, do more than provide a detailed account of obsolete customs; they give the reader the sense of a bitterly divided country in which every event takes on a political significance. The *wappenschaw* is intended as a display of force by the "aristocratical" party supporting the king, but it is also a deliberate outrage of the scruples of the Cameronians—an occasion likely to lead participants and spectators into frivolity and sin. Furthermore, it is an effort by the government "to revive those feudal institutions which united the vassal to the liege lord, and both to the crown." The effort failed, as the narrator ironically observes, because "the youth of both sexes, to whom the pipe and tabor in England, or the bagpipe in Scotland, would have been in themselves an irresistible temptation, were enabled to set them at defiance, from the proud consciousness that they were, at the same time, resisting an act of council," while "The rigour of the strict Calvinists increased, in proportion to the wishes of the government that it should be relaxed."

Arising from the effort of Charles II to establish his authority over the Scottish church by instituting an Episcopalian form of church government, with bishops appointed by the crown, and from the brutal persecution of those who attended services conducted by their own, unauthorized ministers, the dispute, as *Old Mortality* recognizes, had become a class struggle. The aristocracy of Scotland was arrayed on one side and on the other the great majority of the peasantry as well as most of the small middle class and some of the minor landlords. The conflict was national as well, for the Cameronians were protesting against a foreign—English—form of church organization and of worship. Between the two sides lay an uneasy body of moderates who deplored the cruelty and fanaticism of both extremes, or who simply hoped to remain neutral and avoid trouble. The aristocratic party possessed a monopoly of organized military force, but its lack of support among the people and its essential hollowness are comically revealed by Lady Bellenden's raggle-taggle troop of militiamen, consisting of "the fowler and falconer, the footman, and the ploughman at the home farm, with an old drunken cavaliering butler," an ancient steward, and Guse Gibbie, the village half-wit.

In such a society, split by divisions of class, religion, and politics, the position of the moderate is difficult, sometimes impossible. Peaceable men who only want to avoid trouble, sensible and selfish men like Neil Blane, the innkeeper, may survive, but Morton's moderation is based on reason and principle, and his position soon becomes impossible. Both parties watch him—the Presbyterians with special hope because Morton's father had been a notable soldier in their cause during the civil wars—but he is too much aware of their faults to join either one. "Can I be a man and a Scotchman, and look with indifference on that persecution which has made wise men mad?," Morton asks. Then he checks himself with another question: "Who shall warrant me that these people, rendered wild by persecution, would not, in the hour of victory, be as cruel and as intolerant as those by whom they are now hunted down?" And Morton concludes by rejecting both sides: "I am weary of seeing nothing but violence and fury around me—now assuming the mask of lawful authority, now taking that of religious zeal."

Morton's politics are those of the typical Scott hero and of Scott himself, particularly in his fear of the disruptive power of "enthusiasm" (political or religious fanaticism). But Morton is a man ahead of his time, and his principles—the supremacy of law over force, thus guaranteeing the rights and liberty of the subject—will triumph only in the Glorious Revolution of 1688. But he is a man ahead of his time; as the novel shows, there is no place for a moderate in the bitterly divided Scotland of 1679.

Sick of his frustration and inaction, of his dependence on his miserly uncle, of his apparently hopeless love for Edith Bellenden, Morton resolves to win his way as a soldier of fortune on the Continent: "My father's sword is mine, and Europe lies before me." But like most Scott heroes, he is eloquent in making resolutions and slow in carrying them out; he is easily discouraged from executing his plan.

The action of the early chapters forces the reluctant Morton to choose a side—or more accurately, it leaves him no alternative but to join the rebels. After winning a marksmanship contest at the *wappenschaw*—an uncharacteristic act of self-assertion—Morton meets Balfour of Burley, who claims his protection as a friend of his father. Morton is living at Milnwood, the estate of his miserly uncle, and decides to take Burley there. However, he learns that the man he has sheltered is an escaping murderer, the assassin of Archbishop Sharpe, head of the Scottish Episcopal Church. Without realizing it, Morton has made his choice. The royal troopers, commanded by the insolent Sergeant Bothwell, come to Milnwood in their search for the assassin. They do not find him, but they arrest Morton when he claims his rights as a loyal subject, and carry him off to their commander, Claverhouse, who first orders the prisoner to be shot when Morton questions his authority, then revokes his command at the chivalrous appeal of Lord Evandale, Morton's rival for the hand of Edith Bellenden. Carried off a prisoner, Morton is rescued by the Cameronians after they defeat the royal troops. His side has been chosen for him.

The arrival of the king's dragoons at the house of old Milnwood, just at dinner (the noon meal), leads into one of the most powerful and fully developed scenes in any of the Waverley Novels, highly revealing of the characters involved and of the parties that split the country. Dinner, of coarse food and thin beer, is interrupted by a pounding at the gate and by the noisy entrance of the dragoons, with the clatter of their iron-shod boots on the stone floor and the clash of their huge swords. Scott quickly communicates each character's response: old Milnwood's fear of extortion; Morton's apprehension because he has aided a rebel and a murderer; the quandary of old Mause Headrigg, a tenant of Milnwood's, between fear for the life of her son, Cuddie, and the religious zeal that drives her to "testify" against the evils of the time; and the practical Cuddie's use of the confusion to give himself an extra helping of soup.

The tone at first is of rough good humor, as the soldiers force the reluctant Milnwood to prove his loyalty by offering them claret and brandy, but good humor changes to brutal ferocity when Morton questions the authority of Sergeant Bothwell to examine him and Bothwell answers that his broadsword is his commission, then threatens Morton with torture when he refuses to give information about Burley. Tension relaxes briefly when Milnwood offers the troopers a bribe, which Bothwell accepts. But old Mause must express her beliefs, whatever the risk, and as the sergeant begins to administer the oath of loyalty to the household, she breaks out in a furious denunciation of the soldiers: "Malignant adherents ye are to the prelates, foul props to a feeble and filthy cause, bloody beasts of prey, and burdens to the earth." Bothwell cannot overlook that outburst, and Morton is led away under arrest. The scene ends with the expulsion of the Headriggs from Milnwood and the housekeeper's angry judgment of Mause: "Ill-fard, crazy, crack-brained gowk that she is! to set up to be sae muckle better than ither folk, the auld besom."

The scene is an ensemble in which Bothwell, Milnwood, Moreton, both of the Headriggs, and the housekeeper all are given their chance to speak and act. Each has his own style: there is the shrill repetitiousness of Mause ("I wad persevere, natheless, in lifting my testimony against popery, prelacy, antinomianism, erastianism, lapsarianism, sublapsarianism, and the sins and snares of the times"); the rhythmical, poetic intensity that old Milnwood reaches in his agony at risking both his nephew and his money ("O, the lands of Milnwood!—the bonny lands of Milnwood, that have been in the name of Morton twa hundred years! they are barking and fleeing, outfield and infield, haugh and holme!"); the insolent familiarity of Bothwell; and the standard English, as correct as his sentiments, of the hero.

The prevailingly comic tone assures the reader that nothing tragic will occur—old Mause will not be taken out and shot, the hero will not really be tortured—but the comedy is of that nervous kind that rests on apprehension. The mood is carefully varied; tension is high at the entrance of the soldiers, gradually relaxes as they drink Milnwood's liquor, heightens as Morton questions their authority and refuses to reveal the whereabouts of Burley, eases again as Milnwood offers his bribe, then suddenly rises as Mause interrupts with her general denunciation. The reader has waited uneasily for Mause to speak up, hoping she will remain quiet but not really expecting it. Her carefully delayed outburst dramatically reverses mood and action, and leads to Morton's arrest.

Freed by the victors, Morton has no alternative but to join them. His side
has been chosen for him. But he does not prove the fiery rebel that
Claverhouse's words might have led us to expect. The cause is too democratic
and too extreme for a Scott hero to feel comfortable among its supporters.
Morton's first action is to rescue Evandale from a general massacre of prisoners, and his principal concern at the ensuing siege of Tillietudlem is to prevent
the rebels from injuring any of the Bellendens. Characteristically, his doubts
return as soon as he has committed himself; he finds himself "better satisfied
with the general justice of the cause he had espoused, than either with the
measures or the motives of many of those who were embarked in it." The
Scott hero can never be a revolutionary; defeat is always the first eventuality
that occurs to him.

The rebel councils show the factionalism typical of ideological revolutions,
in which, as Scott observes, those expressing the most violent opinions usually "possess and exert the greater degree of energy." Morton, the moderate
man who "would willingly terminate this war without any bloody victory," is
ineffectual and out of place. Among the committed rebels, the novel discriminates precisely between the enthusiasm of Burley, tempered by his ambition
and his recognition of the need for unity; the pure zeal of Macbriar, a Covenanting preacher, admirable yet frightening, untainted by practical considerations; and the bloodthirsty fanaticism of the half-insane Mucklewrath—
"Who speaks of mercy to the bloody house of the malignants? I say take the
infants and dash them against the stones; take the daughters and the mothers
of the house and hurl them from the battlements of their trust, that the dogs
may fatten on their blood."

The rebels enjoy a brief success, occupying Glasgow, but they are divided
among themselves, and their army is routed at Bothwell Bridge, after a useless peace mission by Morton to the Duke of Monmouth, commanding the
royal forces. During his escape, Morton falls in with a band of fugitives, including Macbriar and Mucklewrath. Eager for a scapegoat, they conduct a
drumhead trial and sentence Morton to death; his crimes are his efforts to
save personal friends among the Royalists and to gain honorable terms of
peace. Morton is to die at midnight (the scrupulous Cameronians will not
shed his blood on the Sabbath), but Claverhouse's troopers arrive on the gal-
lop, and the captured rebels, except for Macbriar, are taken out to instant execution just as the impatient Mucklewrath is about to set the clock ahead.

The two extremes, Cameronians and "Malignants" (the Cameronian
name for their persecutors), are personified in their leaders—the passionate
Burley and Claverhouse, the polished, pitiless gentleman. Morton recognizes
a parallel between them in the zeal and ruthlessness of each. "You are very

right," Claverhouse admits, "we are both fanatics: but there is some distinction between the fanaticism of honour and that of dark and sullen superstition." The "fanaticism of honor" can produce an admirable, disinterested courage, but leads also to utter indifference to the lives of others—especially to those of the lower classes. Acknowledging that both he and Burley shed blood "without mercy or remorse," Claverhouse justifies himself: "Surely . . . but of what kind?—There is a difference, I trust, between the blood of learned and reverend prelates and scholars, of gallant soldiers and noble gentlemen, and the red puddle that stagnates in the vein of psalm-singing mechanics, crack-brained demagogues, and sullen boors."

Morton's helplessness as a prisoner brings him relief: "He was now, with respect to his fortune, like a rider who has flung his reins on the horse's neck, and, while he abandoned himself to circumstances, was at least relieved from the task of attempting to direct them"—the typical position of the Scott hero. He is brought before the Privy Council of Edinburgh for judgment, but it has been arranged in advance by Claverhouse that Morton will get off with a sentence of exile. Scott then shows Macbriar resisting questioning and torture. The scene is striking, but at some cost. As an early critic observed, "The contrast of Henry Morton, pardoned by the government and pursuing his fortune in Holland, with Macbriar tortured and put to death, with Burley, a wanderer in the desert hills . . . is almost fatal to the romantic interest of his character."[4] The outraged Morton is *about* to intervene, but, as usual, is prevented.

A gap of ten years follows, for Morton cannot return to Scotland until after the triumph of his Whiggish principles in 1688. The conclusion is melancholy rather than triumphant, as the returning Morton finds all changed, his uncle dead, himself believed drowned, and Edith about to marry Lord Evandale. A confused huddle of events follows as Morton encounters the now half-mad Burley (who refuses to accept the new, moderate government); is discovered by Edith, who breaks her engagement to Evandale; and learns of a plot by Burley against Evandale's life, but characteristically arrives too late to help. A new villain is abruptly introduced when the villainous Basil Oliphant, who has dispossessed the Bellendens, appears and is immediately killed—not by Morton, but by Cuddie Headrigg—and Burley drowns while grappling with a government soldier. Claverhouse, like Burley, cannot accept the new regime and will soon be killed while leading a futile rebellion against it.

In the interest of imaginative truth, Scott feels free to falsify recorded fact, provided that the reader's sense of history is not outraged and the dramatic illusion disturbed; the historical Burley died at sea while returning from exile, but the death that Scott provides seems more appropriate for a man to whom victory is incomplete without the extermination of his enemies. With peace restored and opposing fanaticisms dispelled, the lovers are at last free to marry, enacting in private life the compromise between moderate Whig and moderate Tory achieved in 1688. But there is little joy in their union; they have waited too long. Yet the future belongs to the colorless Morton, so overshadowed in the novel by Burley and Claverhouse. (Moderate men cannot compete with heroic fanatics for the reader's interest.) More accurately, perhaps, the future belongs to what Morton represents—a middle course between opposed and destructive extremes.

Assessment

The author himself remarked, soon after publication, that he preferred *Old Mortality* to any "fictitious narrative" he had "yet been able to produce,"[5] and the book has strong claims to be considered the finest of Scott's historical novels. One notices first the ease and certainty with which a vanished world is re-created—certainly, as Lockhart remarks, that portrayal represents a greater feat of imagination than Scott had ever achieved in his poetry. A Marxist critic, commenting on the Waverley Novels in general, observes that "Like every great popular writer, Scott aims at portraying the totality of national life in its complex interaction between 'above' and 'below.'"[6] That comment applies particularly to *Old Mortality*. The novel is historical in the profoundest sense: its characters are actively engaged in the making of history (against their will, at times!), and their actions and fortunes, even the outcome of their love affairs, are determined by historical events.

Scott is not only concerned with rendering the past, he wishes to interpret it, to relate it to what had gone before and particularly to what would follow. In spite of his exaggerated fear of social disruption in his own time, and his sympathy with Jacobitism and other historical anachronisms, his reading of British history is basically the Whiggish interpretation that became the conventional wisdom of the nineteenth century—in part, surely, through the influence of the Waverley Novels. After 1688, a Great Britain of ordered liberty, free from political and religious fanaticism, from oppression and cruelty, can evolve. This reading of history is most fully expressed in Macaulay's immensely popular *History of England* (actually a history of the events leading up to, and following, the Glorious Revolution of 1688). But Scott's tolerance and wider range of sympathy perhaps enabled the novelist to re-create the past more fairly, and even more accurately, than the historian could do.

But *Old Mortality* can succeed as a historical novel only because it succeeds, first, as a novel. Generations of readers have shared the response of Scott's friend, Lady Louisa Stuart, who found in it an emotional intensity unmatched in the earlier Waverley Novels: "It makes its personages our intimate acquaintance, and its scenes so present to the eye that last night after sitting up unreasonably late over it, I got no sleep, from a kind of fever of mind it had occasioned. It seemed as if I had been an eye and ear witness of all the passages, and I could not lull the agitation into calmness."

As a contemporary reviewer noted, Scott uses historical happenings "rather to develop the characters" of his novels "than for any purposes of political information," and he creates a sense of the past "less by his direct notices of the great transactions . . . than by his casual intimations of their effects on private persons."[7]

Chapter Seven
Rob Roy and Others

Rob Roy, published in January 1818 and named for the notorious Highland outlaw, Rob Roy Macgregor, who plays an important role, enjoyed an even greater success than its predecessors, with a sale of ten thousand copies in two weeks. For many good judges, writes John Buchan, "it has been the favorite among the novels."[1]

Resemblances to *Waverley* are obvious, but differences are likewise important. Again there are Jacobite conspiracies and finally a Jacobite rising; again the hero, Frank Osbaldistone, is a young man with a taste for romance, who dabbles in poetry as well, and who eventually journeys to the Scottish Highlands. But in this novel, the Highlands have no glamour, the Highland life is represented not by a heroic rebel like Fergus MacIvor but by the outlaw Rob Roy, and Frank is promptly disillusioned, and by the end of the novel, he, like Waverley, is happy to subside into the peaceful life of a country gentleman. But Frank's disillusionment counts for less than Waverley's; his romanticism had been superficial in comparison. Interest here is more consistently external, focused on the realities of Highland life rather than on the hero's changing attitudes.

Unlike Waverley, Frank Osbaldistone feels no sympathy for Jacobitism, and his background seems thoroughly bourgeois; his father, a hard-headed businessman (or speculator) with a supreme contempt for poetry, packs his son off to the family seat at Osbaldistone Hall in the north of England, intending to replace him in the firm with his cousin Rashleigh. With Sir Hildebrand Osbaldistone and his loutish sons—all of whom except Rashleigh live for drink, Jacobitism, and hunting—Frank exists in a boredom somewhat relieved by the company of Rashleigh and of the beautiful, mysterious, and daringly unconventional Diana Vernon. (Scott's treatment of the Osbaldistones owes much to Fielding's treatment of drunken country squires.)

Rashleigh goes to London, is left in full charge of the family business while the elder Osbaldistone travels abroad, and absconds with the firm's assets, whatever they may be. The remainder of the novel deals with Frank's efforts to recover those assets, a search that leads him into the Highlands, together with

Bailie Nicol Jarvie, a business associate of his father's, and his rascally servant, the misnamed Andrew Fairservice, who at times plays Sancho Panza to Frank's Don Quixote. After meeting the noted outlaw Rob Roy Macgregor and his intimidating wife, Frank witnesses the defeat of royal troops by the Macgregor clan, and later the escape of Rob Roy from his captors.

Through the influence of Rob Roy and of Diana Vernon, the assets are recovered and the Osbaldistone business is saved. Frank returns to England just as the long-threatened rising breaks out. Sir Hildebrand Osbaldistone and five sons join the rising and, with breathtaking disregard for realism, all of them are disposed of in two pages: one son is killed in a duel, another breaks his neck while trying to jump his horse over a gate, one kills himself in a drinking contest, two are killed in battle, and old Sir Hildebrand, their father, dies of grief. Rashleigh, who has turned informer, is killed by Rob Roy in a duel, and Frank inherits the Osbaldistone estate. The Scott hero invariably comes into an estate by the end of the novel.

The plot, loose and episodic, is seriously flawed by the author's handling of the stolen "assets." First, there is an unconvincing effort to relate the theft to Rashleigh's role as a Jacobite agent—by ruining the Osbaldistone firm he will prevent it from paying off debts to various Highland chieftains, thus increasing economic distress and making the Highlands readier for rebellion. More seriously, the elder Osbaldistone's action in leaving Rashleigh in full charge of affairs for a period of weeks is hopelessly out of character for a man who is described as a hard, shrewd businessman with a keen insight into character, always watchful of his own interests.

Frank had written earlier: "Although I did feel a certain qualm of conscience at having been the means of introducing Rashleigh . . . into my father's business—perhaps his confidence—I subdued it by the reflection that my father was complete master of his own affairs—a man not to be imposed upon, or influenced by anyone." Since that is precisely the impression the reader has formed, the event is incredible; for the sake of his plot, Scott makes his character behave in a way quite contrary to his nature. Nowhere could one find a better illustration of Coleridge's remark that "Scott's great defect" is that "nothing is evolved out of the character or passions of the agent; but all is accident *ab extra* [from the outside]."

The hero of *Rob Roy* is simply a genteel young man with literary inclinations (but this aspect of his characterization is soon forgotten and, unlike the romanticism of Waverley, has almost no influence on the action after the early chapters), almost indistinguishable from other Scott heroes after the opening chapters. The case is different with the heroine, Diana Vernon, who is described as forthright, unconventional, passionate, and witty. Generations of male readers have appropriately fallen in love with her: "Whatever she says or does, we are her devout henchmen, believing fiercely in her beauty, her goodness and her brains."[2] But Diana's speech often belies the intended effect: "No, no Rashleigh, dismiss from your company the false archimage Dissimulation, and it will better ensure your free access to our classical consultations."

Leslie Fiedler's comment seems justified: she is not really the incarnation of romance that she seems, but "only the Good-Bad girl, that stock character of popular fiction . . . . Did she not persuade Frank from the pursuit of poetry, sending him back to protect his father's interests?"[3] Rashleigh, acting as Diana's tutor, has instructed her in philosophy, mathematics, and astronomy (her conversation gives no evidence of such knowledge). The hero comments, with an exquisitely complacent sense of male superiority, that such "profound studies" seemed "more fitted for a churchman than for a beautiful female." Rashleigh's purpose in engaging her in such topics must have been "to break down and confound in her mind the difference and distinction between the sexes, and to habituate her to trains of subtle reasoning, by which he might at his own time invest that which is wrong with the colour of that which is right." Irony does not seem to be intended.

There is much amusing dialogue in the vernacular, a dashing heroine to fall in love with, and—once Frank leaves Osbaldistone Hall to recover the missing assets—striking scenes, with an abundance of adventures, usually occurring in highly picturesque settings. As *Rob Roy's* reception, and its continuing popularity, proved, Scott had produced highly successful entertainment.

The serious significance of *Rob Roy* is found in the Highland-Lowland contrast. As in *Waverley*, the Highlands are Catholic, Jacobite, lawless, and violent; the Lowlands, Protestant, Whiggish, legalistic, and commercial. "Honour," says Bailie Jarvie, the good bourgeois, "is a homicide and a bloodspiller, that gangs about making frays in the street; but Credit is a decent honest man that sits at hame and makes the pat play." There is a noticeable decline in religious fervor from the period of *Old Mortality*, thirty-five years earlier; Jarvie is a devout Presbyterian, certainly—on Sundays, strictly reserving that day for God and the other six for business.

Frank's introduction to the primitive world of the Highlands at the Aberfoil inn is very different from Waverley's, at Glennaquoich. It is an introduction not to an ancient and picturesque tribal life but simply to poverty and squalor, in which pretensions to "honor" cannot help appearing absurd. The "inn" is nothing more than a miserable hut, built of stones and turf, cemented by mud, without even a chimney: "the smoke, having no means to escape but through a hole in the roof, eddied round the rafters of the cottage and hung in sable folds at the height of about five feet from the floor." The door is only "a panel of broken basketwork," and the windows are holes in the wall to let out the smoke from the central fire. Yet the men who are already there, drinking at the only table, feel that their honor has been touched by the intruders, and combat follows—made ridiculous when Bailie Jarvie, unable to get his sword out of its scabbard, holds off his enemy with a red-hot poker and singes a hole in his plaid.

The "battle" of red-coats and Highlanders, when the soldiers are ambushed and defeated at a mountain pass by the old men and boys of Rob Roy's clan, commanded by his wife, Helen, is entirely unheroic, with emphasis on the comic efforts of Bailie Jarvie and Andrew to escape the bullets (Jarvie, in a memorable image, dangles over a cliff, suspended by the skirts of his coat, which had caught on a thorn bush). And there is not even a pretense of "honor" in the execution of a hostage, at Helen MacGregor's orders, and in Scott's presentation of the man's terror, as he tries to clasp the knees of his captors, begs for mercy and life at any cost, under any conditions, is dragged to the edge of a high bank above a lake, crying out for help, and then, with a great stone tied to his neck, is thrown into the lake "with a loud halloo of vindictive triumph, above which, however, the last death-shriek . . . was distinctly heard." The effect is not even destroyed by the heroic rant of Helen MacGregor: "'I could have bid you live,' she said, 'had life been to you the same weary and wasting burden that it is to me—that it is to every noble and generous mind. But you—wretch! you could creep through the world unaffected by its various disgraces, its ineffable miseries, its constantly accumulating masses of crime and sorrow,'" etc.

Scott's historical realism has intensified. Overpopulation and resulting poverty, not picturesque tradition, shape the society of the Highlands. In *Rob Roy*, economics determines history, and the Highlands, consequently, appear far less romantic than when seen through Waverley's eyes. Nothing could be less romantic than one important cause of discontent; George I has discontinued the royal pensions to the clan chiefs. Human possibilities now seem narrowly limited; the power of choice hardly exists. "Historical forces appear more implacable . . . but at the same time Scott's sympathy for the human beings involved in the drama of history deepens,"[4] as a recent critic observes.

The Black Dwarf

The Black Dwarf and *A Legend of Montrose* (1819) are the shortest and by general agreement the weakest of the "Scotch novels." The only novelty in

The Black Dwarf is in its title character, who, to quote a contemporary review, "is a deformed misanthrope; who having been betrayed in a love affair by his bosom friend, retires in disgust to a wild waste, called Mucklestane Muir, where he builds himself a hut, and from the singularity of his person, dress, and deportment, is taken by the ignorant country-people for a supernatural being, who holds converse with the devil and familiar spirits, and has unlimited power over the fortunes and fates of all who live in his neighbourhood."[5] The narrative, as Scott himself commented in his review of *The Black Dwarf* and *Old Mortality*, "abounds with plots, elopements, ravishments, and rescues, and all the violent events which are so common in romance, and of such rare occurrence in real life."[6] As for the hero and the heroine, Scott devastatingly remarks, they excite no interest at all, "being just that sort of *pattern* people whom nobody cares a farthing about."[7] But, Scott adds, if the reader can tolerate the plot, "he will find the work itself contains passages both of natural pathos and fantastic terror."[8]

The setting is the Border in 1707, once again a time when a Jacobite rising is threatened. The most interesting novelty is in the satirical realism with which the motives of the conspirator's motives are presented as they encourage themselves with liquor:

"Our commerce is destroyed," hallowed old John Rewcastle, A Jedburgh smuggler, from the lower end of the table.

"Our agriculture is ruined," said the Laird of Broken-girth-flow, a territory which, since the days of Adam, had borne nothing but ling and whortle-berries.

"Our religion is cut up, root and branch," said the pimple-nosed pastor of the Episcopal meeting-house at Kirk whistle.

"We shall shortly neither dare shoot a deer nor kiss a wench without a certificate from the presbytery and kirk-treasurer," said Marischal Wells.

"Or make a brandy jeroboam in a frosty morning without license from a commissioner of the excise," said the smuggler.

"Or ride over the fell in a moonless night," said Westburnflat, "without asking leave of young Earnscliff or some Englified justice of the peace. Thae were gude days on the Border when there was neither peace nor justice heard of."

The principal interest of the work lies in the character of the Dwarf, in whom some critics, beginning with Lockhart, have discovered a unique revelation of Scott's inner life. *The Black Dwarf*, Lockhart writes melodramatically, "derives a singular interest from its delineation of the dark feelings so often connected with physical deformity; feelings which appear to have diffused their shadow over the whole genius of Byron—and which, but for this single picture, we should hardly have conceived ever to have passed through Scott's happier mind. All the bitter blasphemy of spirit which, from infancy to the tomb, swelled up in Byron . . . all this black and desolate train of reflections must have been encountered and deliberately subdued by the manly parent of the Black Dwarf."⁹ And Lockhart's opinion is supported by a curious coincidence: on first reading *The Black Dwarf*, Byron's half-sister, Augusta Leigh, was convinced that her brother had written it.

But there is no evidence anywhere in Scott's writings, even in his letters and journals, that he responded to his lameness with Byronic bitterness. Even if he had, he was the last writer to reveal such intimate feelings to the public, or to exhibit before the world, as Matthew Arnold wrote of Byron, "the pageant of his bleeding heart." But the most convincing evidence can be found in the Dwarf's language: "'Common humanity,' exclaimed the being, with a scornful laugh that sounded like a shriek, 'where got ye that catch-word—that noose for woodcocks—that common disguise for mantraps—that bait which the wretched idiot who swallows will soon find covers a hook with barbs ten times sharper than those you lay for the animals which you murder for your luxury!'" Surely this is conventional rant, not private confession, and the Dwarf himself is a stock type, an experiment in the Byronic mode so fashionable at the time.

A Legend of Montrose

A Legend of Montrose is set entirely in the Scottish Highlands in 1644, a time when the earl of Montrose led a rising of Highland clans against the Scottish government, which supported the Parliamentary side in the English civil wars. Montrose's rebellion, with its almost incredible series of victories against great odds and its sudden crushing defeat, might have provided a striking subject, but Scott largely ignores the historical events. His plot is concerned with a triangle involving the usual genteel hero and heroine and the Highlander Allan M'Aulay, who believes himself to be gifted with the second sight. Interest derives principally from Allan's prophecy that the hero, his rival in love and former friend, will be stabbed by a Highlander whose identity Allan cannot foretell. The stabbing occurs, but the hero recovers—the assailant is Allan himself.

Of the characters, Dugald Dalgetty, the Lowland soldier of fortune, attracts attention at least partly because he is the only figure in the novel to speak a vernacular Scots. The Gaelic of the Highlanders is rendered in pseudo-poetic diction resembling the speech of Fenimore Cooper's Indians in his *Leatherstocking Tales*—a literary influence can certainly be traced:

"'Kenneth,' said the old outlaw, 'hear the last words of the sire of thy father. A Saxon soldier and Allan of the Red Hand left this camp within these few hours, to travel to the country of Caberfae. Pursue them as the bloodhound pursues the hurt deer, swim the lake, climb the mountain, thread the forest, tarry not until you join them.'"

In the tragedy of Allan M'Aulay, who believes himself gifted with the second sight and (unknowingly) foresees his own treacherous attempt to murder a friend, Scott treats a subject similar to that of *Guy Mannering*, or at least of the beginning of *Guy Mannering*, but again is unable to deal with it seriously because he seems unable to decide whether or not to accept supposedly supernatural powers at face value or to explain them rationally as due either to coincidence or to a deranged imagination.

But one does not read *A Legend of Montrose* to learn whether or how Allan's prophecies will be fulfilled; one reads to get more of Major Dalgetty. The character seems derived principally from Shakespeare's Fluellen(a military pedant) and from the memoirs of two seventeenth-century Scottish mercenaries, Colonel Robert Monro and Sir James Turner. To these sources might be added, as Buchan suggests, a dash of Ben Jonson's Bobadil in *Every Man in His Humour* and the *miles gloriosus* (braggart soldier) in general; of Smollett's Lismahago in *Humphrey Clinker*; and above all of Shakespeare's Falstaff, in Dalgetty's devotion to food and drink, and in the cynical realism with which he views his trade of war. But all characters in fiction are composites, and if the elements from which Dalgetty is composed are not original, the final product most certainly is. The mixture of unscrupulousness, selfishness, vanity, pedantry, religious cant, and shrewd realism displayed in his speeches is entirely individual:

I have heard enough since I came here to satisfy me that a cavalier of honour is free to take any part in this civil embroilment whilk he may find most convenient for his own peculiar. "Loyalty" is your password, my lord; "Liberty," roars another chield . . . . "The King," shouts one war-cry; "The Parliament," roars another; "Montrose for ever," cries Donald, waving his bonnet . . . . "Fight for the bishops," says a priest, with his gown and rochet; "Stand stout for the Kirk," cries a minister, in a Geneva cap and band—good watchwords all—excellent watchwords. Whilk cause is the best I cannot say. But sure am I that have fought knee-deep in blood many a day for that was ten degrees worse than the words of them all.

That speech not only characterizes Dalgetty but satirizes all the inspiring slogans for which men kill. Dalgetty may be a "flat" character, to use E. M. Forster's term—a character that does not develop or change. But the reader is entirely satisfied to see how, like Falstaff, he extricates himself from every pre-dicament. If not the most original, he is certainly one of the richest of Scott's comic characters. Paradoxically, the humor of Dalgetty provides the most serious interest of *A Legend of Montrose.*

Chapter Eight
The Heart of Midlothian

The Heart of Midlothian (originally *Tales of My Landlord*, second series) was published in four volumes, instead of the usual three, in July of 1818, about six months after *Rob Roy*. A letter to Scott from his friend Lady Louisa Stuart indicates its immediate and extraordinary success: "I have not only read it myself, but am in a house where everybody is tearing it out of each other's hands, and talking of nothing else . . . . Had this story been conducted by a common hand, Effie would have attracted all our concern and sympathy—Jeanie only cold approbation. Whereas Jeanie, without youth, beauty, genius, warm passions, or any other novel-perfection, is here our object from beginning to end. This is 'enlisting the affections in the cause of virtue' ten times more than ever Richardson did."[1]

The success of *Midlothian* has continued, and a good many critics (especially, perhaps, those who do not admire the Waverley Novels in general) have considered it Scott's finest work. One reason for this preference is negative—the absence of the genteel hero and heroine. The novel really has no hero, since George Staunton, Effie Deans's seducer, is half-villain, and Reuben Butler, the lover and later husband of Effie's sister Jeanie, plays a minor role. Lady Stuart's comment on the moral value of *The Heart of Midlothian* indicates another important reason for its nineteenth-century popularity: a book containing characters like Jeanie Deans and her father David would do much to overcome lingering suspicions of novel reading as a frivolous and morally suspect activity. Similarly, some twentieth-century critics have found that Jeanie's moral dilemma, of whether or not to save her sister's life by a lie, gives *Midlothian* a seriousness lacking elsewhere in Scott.

The story is based on the history of an actual woman, Helen Walker, whose sister had been convicted of infanticide, like Effie Deans, and who saved her sister's life in exactly the way that Jeanie Deans would save Effie, by journeying alone to London and making a personal appeal to the queen. Scott opens his novel in 1737. David Deans, an intensely pious cowfeeder, or dairy farmer—"a poor, rude, vulgar milkman," said one class-conscious reviewer—living near Edinburgh, has two daughters, Effie and Jeanie. Effie, the younger and more beautiful, is seduced and made pregnant by Sir

George Staunton, a dissipated young Englishman of good family who has become deeply involved with criminals. She is able to hide her condition from her sister and father—on Jeanie's rare visits, she sees Effie in the darkness of the shop—and even from her employers. The wife is sick and bedridden, and the absent-minded husband notices nothing. "Neighbors and fellow-servants," adds Scott, "remarked with malicious curiosity . . . the disfigured shape, loose dress, and pale cheeks" of Effie, "but to no one would she grant her confidence." Under a harsh law of the time, since Effie has informed no one of her condition and cannot produce the child, she is assumed to have murdered it to conceal her guilt and is sentenced to death. In fact, the baby has been stolen by Staunton's demented former mistress while Effie lay sick.

Jeanie could save her sister's life by declaring that Effie had told her of her condition, but Jeanie will not lie, and Effie is sentenced to hang. Jeanie then travels alone to London to appeal to the queen, and with the help of the Duke of Argyle obtains a royal interview and a pardon for Effie. Effie eventually becomes rich and a great lady by marrying Staunton. Jeanie, her father, and her husband (she has married Reuben Butler) are befriended by Argyle and live out their lives contentedly on his estate in the Highlands, where they prosper, thanks to Argyle's generosity and Effie's generous gifts. Effie, however, can never be happy. Staunton is killed many years later by his own son, now a Highland outlaw, (father and son are unknown to each other), who then flees to America and joins an Indian tribe. Sin must be punished.

The Heart of Midlothian falls into four distinct sections. Chapters 2–7 deal with the riot during which a mob captures Tolbooth Prison and lynches the hated Captain Porteous; chapters 8–24 are concerned primarily with the trial and condemnation of Effie and with Jeanie's moral dilemma; chapters 25–39 are concerned with Jeanie's journey to London and her efforts to win the pardon; chapters 40–52 show Jeanie's marriage, her settlement at Argyle's estate and her prosperity there, the marriage of Effie and George Staunton, and Staunton's death. But critical praise has centered on the second part, seventeen chapters out of fifty-two.

The description of the Porteous riot is only tenuously connected with the central action: Staunton is supposed to have incited the riot in the hope of rescuing Effie from prison. Thematically it is more relevant, revealing both the savage severity and the inner corruption of the system of "justice" that has condemned Effie to death. Part 3—the journey to London and the obtaining of the pardon—by general agreement shows a considerable falling off of interest. Jeanie is no longer a free agent and consequently is less interesting. She is kidnapped by outlaws, then rescued by a madwoman, and when she arrives in London her affairs are largely managed by the Duke of Argyle. Yet the

novel could hardly have ended with the conviction of Effie. Jeanie, not Effie,
is the center of interest, and her journey to London and her interview with the
queen are the natural consequences, given her boldness and determination, of
her refusal to lie at Effie's trial. And what would the reader's impression of
Jeanie be if Effie had been hanged for the sake of her sister's conscience?

The final section, which has no basis in the story of Helen Walker, who
died in poverty, seems to have no real function except to reward the virtuous
and punish the wicked. Scott's motive for writing this epilogue seems to have
been purely commercial. In November 1817 he had contracted for a still un-
written, unplanned and even unthought of work to be published in four volumes, which could be sold for a considerably higher price, and he had used
the advance to pay off a large debt. Consequently, the fourth volume had to
be written, whether his story required it or not.

Critics have justified their preference for *The Heart of Midlothian* by finding in it a thematic significance that provides a degree of unity and seriousness not found in any other of the Waverley Novels. Robin Mayhead begins
his analysis with a full admission of what he considers to be Scott's normal
slackness: "Inconsistencies of plot and character, internal contradiction,
anachronisms," seem not to have troubled either Scott or his readers. But in
The Heart of Midlothian, at least, "if only for one half its length, Scott is sufficiently mastered by a theme to be inspired to a piece of almost entirely consis-
tent artistic achievement." That theme is a question—"What does human
justice amount to?"[2]

But the argument overlooks the fact that except by implication, in the description of the Porteous riot, the novel really contains no serious questioning
either of the particular law that condemns Effie, or of the whole legal
machine—nothing in fact but Mrs. Saddletree's half-humorous comment
that "if the law makes murders, the law should be hanged for them; or if they
wad hang a lawyer instead, the country wad find nae faut." Neither does the
novel ever question the fact that Effie, who is guilty of nothing worse than
unchastity, can be saved from hanging only by an arbitrary exercise of royal
authority. That is simply a necessary condition of the action.

David Craig, in his *Scottish Literature and the Scottish People*, proposes
that the moral and religious feeling of Scottish Presbyterianism, above all the
moral scruples of its believers, is the true subject of *Midlothian*—at least in
chapters 9–19, which Craig considers to be the heart of the work. Much justi-
fication can be found for this view, for in no other Scott novel are the actions
of the principal character so consistently controlled by religious belief. Even
in *Old Mortality*, dealing with the revolt of Presbyterian extremists against
the government of Charles II, the hero, Morton, seems not to be influenced

in the least by religious considerations and considers the peculiar beliefs and
behavior of his fellow rebels simply as proof of their "enthusiasm" or fanaticism. Certainly *Old Mortality* contains nothing comparable, in its insight into
the feelings of the Scottish people, to a minor scene in *The Heart of
Midlothian*, when Effie, returning from a dance at the late hour of eight in
the evening, meets her sister. Effie is singing a verse from an old ballad, belonging to an older but not forgotten time, when Scotland was not yet
Presbyterian:

> The elfin knight sate on the brae,
>   The broom grows bonny, the broom grows fair;
> And by there came lilting a lady so gay,
>   And we daurna gang doun to the broom nae mair.

Such ballads end in seduction, as Jeanie knows, and she is still more shocked
when the suddenly repentant Effie declares that "if there were as mony dances
the morn's night as there are merry dancers in the north firmament on a
frosty e'en, I winna budge an inch to gang near ane of them." (Dancing itself
is of course a sin in the eyes of David Deans, and probably Jeanie's too.)
David Deans enters, and sternly forbids dancing, along with all other "disso-
lute pastimes." Effie, half resentful and half repentant, decides not to confess
the whole truth to her sister, that she had "danced wi' him [Staunton] four
times on the green down-bye"—to admit so much would give Jeanie the
upper hand: "she wad by mistress and more." Instead, Effie makes a resolution, of a kind that can never be kept: "But I'll no gang back there again. I'm
resolved I'll no gang back. I'll lay in a leaf of my Bible, and that's very near as
I had made an aith, that I winna gang back." As Craig observes, "We see that
religion touches these people all round, strengthening Jeanie, chafing
Effie—for the best she can do live up to the religion of her community is
these pathetic resolves to 'be good.'"[3]

But Jeanie Deans is the central figure of *Midlothian*, and her scruples, her
refusal to lie, and her faith in a providential ordering of events—which gives
her courage to undertake the journey to London and confidence that she will
succeed—all spring from her religious faith. Her father, David Deans, is
given a touching scriptural eloquence at times, as when he speaks of his grief
for his dead wife: "She's not to be forgotten on this side of time, but He that
gives the wound can send the ointment . . . . I have been this night on the
banks of Ulai, plucking an apple here and there." Yet Deans is an archetype
of the sectarian spirit—a hair-splitter, a quibbler, a dogmatist who has perfect confidence in his own infallibility and in his unique capacity to thread his

way safely between "right-hand snares and extremes and left-hand wayslidings," an ideologue of a kind still familiar in the twentieth century.

"I am not a MacMillanite, or a Russellite, or a Hamiltonian, or a Harleyite, or a Howdenite," he declares; but he is a Deansite, a sect having one member, or possibly two. "Though I will neither exalt myself nor pull down others, I wish every man and woman in this land had kept the true testimony, and the middle and straight path, as it were, on the ridge of a hill . . . as weel as Johnny Dodds of Farthing's Acre, and ae man mair that shall be nameless."

The spiritual pride revealed in that speech is breathtaking. "That is as much as to say," observes one of his listeners, "that Johnny Dodds of Farthing's Acre, and David Deans of St. Leonards, constitute the only members of the true, real, unsophisticated Kirk of Scotland?" Deans's disclaimer is conventional and unconvincing: "God forbid that I suld make sic a vainglorious speech, when there are sae mony professing Christians!" He is no hypocrite, but his religion has lost contact with reality. When his daughter Effie, a beautiful and willful girl, goes off to take service in Edinburgh, her father is concerned only that she may be seduced by false doctrine. The possibility of a literal seduction never occurs to him. When Jeanie seeks his guidance, he can think only of his absurd scruples about whether or not his daughter should recognize the existing government by testifying in court—leaving Jeanie to face alone the basic moral issue of whether a lie can ever be justified. Her concern is always for behavior, his for doctrine.

But a sense of the "Presbyterian ethos" is not enough in itself to provide unity and coherence throughout a four-volume novel. The structural flaws remain; most of the critical praise for *The Heart of Midlothian* has actually been praise for chapters 8–24 (ending with Effie's condemnation) or 8–28, when Jeanie sets out for London. It could also be argued that Scott finally evades the moral issue, since Jeanie's decision to tell the truth does not, after all, cost her sister's life. (But Shakespeare avoided a similar issue in *Measure for Measure*, a play with which *Midlothian* invites comparison. After Isabella has refused to buy her brother's life by sacrificing her virginity to Angelo, the viceroy, the Duke himself, appears and sets everything to rights.)

More seriously, Scott never actually renders the process by which Jeanie makes her decision. "O father, we are cruelly sted between God's law and man's laws—what shall we do?," she exclaims; but in a single paragraph of logical argument, Scott has her arrive at her decision. The sense of Jeanie's pain and uncertainty, which the reader must have to acquit her of a self-righteous concern for her own conscience at the expense of her sister's life, is not given. Scott does not command a language supple enough to render the flux of Jeanie's thoughts and emotions. Instead, he gives us exposition and a simile: she is "tossed, in short, like a vessel in an open roadstead, during a storm, and, like that vessel, resting on one only sure cable and anchor,—faith in Providence, and a resolution to discharge her duty." Perhaps Scott could have done no more; the novel had not yet evolved to the point where it could offer not merely a logical analysis of decision-making in a particularly difficult case, but could present the agonized *process*.

But the significance of *The Heart of Midlothian* probably lies at least as much in its contribution to the development of the English novel as in its own achievement. Only in *Midlothian* does Scott make a person of the lower classes, speaking in Scots, the central figure of a novel—and Jeanie is a good deal more central than the conventional heroes and heroines of the other Waverley Novels. For an intelligent contemporary reviewer, the real interest of the work lay in its "representation of rustic and homely characters;—and not in the ludicrous or contemptuous representation of them—but by making them at once more natural and more interesting than they had ever been before in any work of fiction."[4] That is true, and the reviewer might have been more explicit. He might have added that never before had a person of Jeanie's class been made the protagonist of a long and serious novel. *The Heart of Midlothian* helped to make possible, for example, George Eliot's *Adam Bede* and Thomas Hardy's *Tess of the D'Urbervilles*; it opened a new range of subject matter and of character for the novelist.

Chapter Nine
The Bride of Lammermoor

The Bride of Lammermoor is stark tragedy, the only one of the Waverley Novels in which the implications of the plot are allowed to work themselves out to the full. Here, no Colonel Talbot or Meg Merrilies intervenes to save the hero from the consequences of his actions, no real or surrogate parent restores him to his lost inheritance, and the heroine is involved in the hero's doom. Edgar Ravenswood, with his dark and often sullen countenance, incessantly brooding on the wrongs done to his family, appears far removed from Waverley or the nearly anonymous young men of *Guy Mannering* and *The Antiquary*.

Lucy Ashton, with her beauty and her "softness of spirit" that "seemed closely allied to feebleness of mind," seems the typical blonde heroine, submissive and proper. She characterizes herself with the song she sings to her lute, at her first appearance:

> Look not thou on beauty's charming,
> Sit thee still when kings are arming,
> Taste not when the wine-cup glistens,
> Speak not when the people listens,
> Stop thine ear against the singer,
> From the red gold keep thy finger,
> Vacant heart, and hand, and eye,
> Easy live and quiet die.

But the submissive Lucy stabs her bridegroom on her wedding night, and we last see her hiding in the corner of the huge fireplace in her bridal apartment, "her night-clothes torn and dabbled with blood, her eyes glazed," pointing her bloody fingers at her mother and brother, as she says, "with a sort of grinning exultation," "So, you have ta'en up your bonny bridegroom?" Lucy dies in her madness, and Ravenswood perishes in the Kelpie's Flow, a quicksand on the seashore, while riding furiously toward a duel with her brother—thus fulfilling an ancient prophecy:

> When the last Laird of Ravenswood to Ravenswood shall ride,
> And woo a dead maiden to be his bride,

He shall stable his steed in the Kelpie's flow,
And his name shall be lost for evermoe!

This tragic intensity seems so remarkable that a biographical-critical myth
has been created to account for it—*The Bride of Lammermoor* was not a product of Scott's normal mind. He suffered from a severe illness, seeming to
threaten his life, in the winter and spring of 1819, and, writes his most recent
biographer, "Page after page was written in a blurred trance of suffering in
which he did not know what words he was putting down, images and dreamlike actions rising somehow out of unconscious depths of the imagination
while he himself struggled through a drugged nightmare world."[1] But the
manuscript is written in Scott's normal hand, showing no trace of illness. In
fact, it seems probable that Scott had nearly completed his manuscript before
he became dangerously sick. There is no biographical reason, then, to set *The
Bride of Lammermoor* apart from the rest of Scott's work. The story is based
on fact; by his choice of subject, Scott had committed himself to tragedy. He
had saturated himself in Border history, often bloody and disastrous; he had
begun his career as a collector of ballads, and the ballad view of life is essentially tragic. What is surprising is not that Scott wrote a tragic novel, but that
he wrote only one.

Edgar is the only survivor of an ancient, proud, and turbulent house.
Staunch Tories, loyal to their king, the Ravenswoods have taken the losing
side in the political struggles of their time and have paid a heavy price. The
title has been abolished—Edgar is the "Master of Ravenswood" only by
courtesy—and through obscure legal and financial manipulations, the estate
has been lost to the patiently scheming Sir William Ashton, one of the victorious Whigs. The Lord Keeper—his official title—is a man of the new order,
a cunning lawyer and politician, "a skillful fisher in the troubled waters of a
state divided by factions and delegated by authority." Scott may pretend that
"whether he [Ashton] had given him [the old Lord Ravenswood] good cause
for enmity" was doubtful, but the reader is left in no doubt that the wealthy
and influential Ashton, trained in the law, has involved his victim in "legal
toils and pecuniary snares."

The Ashtons now live in Ravenswood Castle; only the half-ruined tower of
Wolf Crag is left to Edgar. There the novel opens with the funeral ceremonies
for the old Lord Ravenswood, Edgar's father, attended by all their kinsmen.
The ceremony, conducted according to the forbidden Anglican rites, is interrupted by an officer of the law followed by armed men. But he is helpless
when Edgar draws his sword, ordering the service to continue, and the whole

company supports him. In his anger at this persecution, Edgar pronounces his curse on Sir William: "it was only he that dug the grave who could have the mean cruelty to disturb the obsequies; and Heaven do as much to me and more, if I requite not to this man and his house the ruin and disgrace he has brought on me and mine!" That curse will be fulfilled.

Feudal tradition requires a wake, regardless of poverty, and a wake follows: "The tables swam in wine, the populace feasted in the courtyard . . . and two years' rent of Ravenswood's remaining property hardly defrayed the charge of the funeral revel." Only Edgar does not join in the drinking—he is alone, as he is throughout the novel. At last his relations leave, "with deep protestations—to be forgotten on the morrow," if remembered at all.

Without lands or tenants or money, left bankrupt by this absurd ceremony, Edgar plans to emigrate, perhaps to join the Jacobite cause in France (the period is the first decade of the eighteenth century), or to carve out a career as a soldier of fortune. But he determines first to "expostulate" with Sir William Ashton—an intention likely to lead to violence, even murder. Instead, he saves the lives of Sir William and of Lucy with a well-aimed shot when he sees a wild bull charging them as they walk in the forest.

Lucy's gentle beauty is irresistible to Ravenswood, while she is fascinated by his dark intensity. Cunning Sir William recognizes the mutual attraction and encourages it; he feels an obligation, and he senses a coming change in the political situation in which a reconciliation between the families, even a marriage, might be to his interest. Apparently with her father's encouragement, Lucy and Edgar meet, and when Edgar is sent abroad on an undefined diplomatic or political mission, they pledge undying loyalty to each other. He breaks a coin in two and each one takes a half, as a token of their love—Lucy with the qualification that while she will never marry anyone but Edgar, neither will she marry anyone against the will of her parents.

But their love is doomed. Sir William stands in awe of his proud and domineering wife, "endowed by nature with strong powers and violent passions," who stimulates her husband's ambition and greed, playing Lady Macbeth to his vacillating Macbeth. She holds an unquenchable hatred for the Ravenswood family, and when she returns from a long journey she refuses to recognize her daughter's engagement and finds a husband for her, Arthur Bucklaw—who is all the readier because he holds an imagined grievance against Ravenswood. Their letters to each other are intercepted, but Edgar returns just as Lucy and Bucklaw are to be betrothed, and insists on hearing from her own mouth that she wishes to be freed from their pledge. But Lady Ashton is present, and Lucy cannot bring herself to defy her mother. After denouncing her for her treachery, Edgar scornfully gives her his half of the broken coin, and the story moves quickly to its catastrophe.

Catastrophe is foreseen from the outset, and its shape becomes clear with the first meeting of Edgar and Lucy. Young lovers of hostile families—with that meeting, *Romeo and Juliet* inevitably comes to mind. Here too are a pair of star-crossed lovers. The differences are significant, of course. Lucy is no Juliet, ready to invite her lover into her bedroom—an impossibility in a Waverley Novel—or to abandon her family and run any risk to be reunited with him. And if only Friar Laurence's letter to Romeo had not been delayed, or if Juliet had awakened a few minutes earlier as she lay drugged in the tomb, the two lovers could have escaped together. They are beaten by unlucky accidents.

But the odds are heavier against Edgar and Lucy: "star-crossed" here has a deeper meaning. They meet at all only by the most improbable of accidents, and only the temporary effect of that accident on Sir William allows their love to flourish. But the reader is always conscious of insuperable obstacles, knowing exactly how and when they will take effect. And even if, by miracle (the sudden death of Lady Ashton, for example), their marriage had been possible, a happy ending is inconceivable. Certainly a marriage between Edgar and Lucy would hardly constitute a happy ending, given their totally different personalities and backgrounds, their opposite political and religious opinions (Anglican and Presbyterian) at a time of bitter political and religious conflict. Montagues and Capulets may have hated each other, but they were essentially alike.

And Edgar's position, if he had married into the family that had usurped his own rights, would have been unbearable. As old Alice, a former retainer of the Ravenswoods, warns him: "Are you prepared to sit lowest at the board which was once your father's own, unwillingly, as a connexion and ally of his proud successor? Are you ready to live on his bounty . . . . Can you say as Sir William Ashton says, think as he thinks, vote as he votes, and call your father's murderer your worshipful father-in-law and revered patron?"

If Lucy is the typical Scott heroine, passive even in her deepest love, Ravenswood—"brimming with passionate interiority," as one critic puts it—seems strikingly different from the earlier heroes. At his first appearance, "with dark and sullen brow," at his father's funeral, he vows to repay to Sir William and his house "the ruin and disgrace he has brought on me and mine!" (As he does, in a way he could never have foreseen.) In his love for Lucy, he seems to be almost helplessly drawn, against his own knowledge of all the barriers, internal as well as external. Like Brown's rescue of Dinmont, or Lovel's of Sir Arthur and Isabella Wardour, that curse, and the killing of the bull, are the only dramatic actions he undertakes before his return from his mission abroad. (He fights a duel that is forced upon him, and spares his opponent; the Waverley hero does not kill; he saves.) Nevertheless he is more strongly individual than any of the earlier heroes, and unlike them he is truly a protagonist, a central figure in his own novel.

The Ravenswoods have been men of the sword; Sir William is a man of papers. We first see him in his library, at Ravenswood Castle, preparing to undo his enemy: "On the massive oaken table and reading-desk lay a confused mass of letters, petitions, and parchments; to toil amongst which was the pleasure at once and the plague of Sir William Ashton's life." He is listening to an account of what had passed at the funeral of old Lord Ravenswood, of the threats that had been made against himself, the perhaps treasonable toasts that had been drunk, the defiance of legal authority, taking careful notes to support any accusation he might make, confident "that he was now master of the remaining fortune, and even of the personal liberty, of young Ravenswood." And even of his life—there may be grounds for a charge of treason. (Again we see the conflict between an order based on tradition, on personal relationships and even on personal violence, and one based on law and contract.) It is while the Lord Keeper walks abroad to consider his course of action, that Edgar saves his life— avoiding a confrontation that would probably have ended in Ashton's death or serious injury, and Edgar's lifelong exile.

Open violence, then, has been replaced by law, but not by justice. The English compromise that Scott profoundly admires, the combination of order and liberty, with full protection for the rights and property of the subject, does not yet exist in Scotland. The law is the weapon of the strongest faction, enriching its members with the property of their enemies. Impartial justice cannot be had. Idealists may look forward to a time when justice shall be open to Whig and Tory alike, but in Scotland that time has not yet come, although Edgar could appeal his case to the English House of Lords. There he might win, since a judgment would be based on equity rather than technicalities. Sir William knows this, which gives him a powerful motive for conciliating his enemy, even beyond his fear of a violent revenge. For Sir William Ashton is a timid man, except when among his papers.

Sir William is a new man as well, with no roots in the countryside, while the Ravenswoods have held Ravenswood Castle for nearly five hundred years. But the past is viewed with unsentimental clarity. Edgar's father, says one of his former tenants, had lost everything because he "guided his gear like a fule," without even making provision for those who depended upon him, and who were left in poverty in their old age. And the peasants who have gained their freedom from the oppressive feudal dues have no reason to be sorry for the change. Their judgment is unequivocal and harsh: "When they [the Ravenswoods] had lands and power, they were ill guides of them baith, and now their head's down, there's few care how long they may be of lifting them."

The reader is given one glimpse of that "heroic" and violent past through the story of a former tenant who had gone out with the feudal militia to fight for the king at Bothwell Bridge (where Henry Morton had fought on the opposite side, in *Old Mortality*):

Into the water we behoved a' to splash, heels ower head, ae horse driving on anither . . . the very bushes on the ither side were ableeze with Whig guns; and my horse had just taen the grund, when a black-avised westland carle—I wad mind the face o' him a hundred years yet—clapped the end of his long black gun within a quarter's length of my lug! [ear]. By the grace o' Mercy, the horse swerved round, and I fell aff at the tae side as the ball whistled by at the tither, and the auld lord took the Whig such a swauk wi' his broadsword that he made twa pieces o' his head, and down fell the lurdane wi' a' his bouk abune me.

A moment of war is intensely imagined here, thanks to the use of Scots instead of English.

One character, above all, represents the past—Caleb Balderstone, the last servant of the Ravenswoods, faithful to his masters to the end. Trying to keep house at Wolf's Crag without food or money or fuel or furniture, incessantly inventing new lies and excuses to hide his master's poverty, making frantic efforts to play on the lingering loyalty of former Ravenswood tenants, Caleb provides both comedy and pathos. Constantly looking back to "the gude auld times, when authority had its right," when "A vassal scarce held a calf or a lamb his ain, till he had first asked if the Lord of Ravenswood was pleased to accept it," and must even ask the lord's consent before marrying ("and mony a merry tale they tell about that right"), he is the family past embodied, absurd yet inescapable, freezing Edgar in his feudal role, holding him to his traditional loyalties. Here there is no escape, as there had been in *Old Mortality*, into a more fortunate era.

The Bride of Lammermoor is a novel haunted by the past. Edgar is more enlightened, more intelligent, more aware of the consequences of his actions, than anyone else in the novel, yet his position is fatally circumscribed. Poor and powerless, burdened by a sense of familial obligation and tradition (revenge) which he can neither accept nor throw off, influenced by the fatalism and superstition of the Scottish countryside, he cannot escape from his heritage. Like a character in an old ballad, he must live his tragic story of true love thwarted, concluding in madness for one of the lovers and death for them both. It is a story whose outcome he partly foresees, but cannot change—by loving Lucy, he chooses his doom, and at times seems to know what he does.

The supernatural—witches, apparitions, prophecies, omens, and warnings—hovers continuously on the fringes of this story. It is appropriate to time and place, to still-powerful folk tradition, and to the ballad tradition that fascinated Scott. It imparts deeper significance to characters and action, it reinforces the reader's sense of impending doom. Almost at the outset, old Caleb recites the cryptic prophecy of the Kelpie's flow—and the experienced reader will expect that prophecy to be fatally fulfilled. After his rescue of Sir William and Lucy, Edgar carries the helpless Lucy to a nearby "fountain," or spring, the "Mermaiden's Well." There, according to legend, a lord of Ravenswood had once met a beautiful and unknown young woman. They met often, but always by the fountain—until Lord Raymond rashly tried to learn the secret of her identity, when with a shriek she plunged into the fountain and disappeared forever, while bubbles stained with blood rise to the surface. Some rationalized the story by saying that Lord Raymond had met his mistress there, a woman of lower rank, and had murdered her for infidelity. But whether accepting the legend literally or not, "All . . . agreed that the spot was fatal to the Ravenswood family."

There also, by the "fated fountain," Lucy and Edgar hold their decisive interview, before his departure for France, when Ravenswood intends to bid Lucy farewell, but which ends instead by their declaring their love and confirming their engagement with oaths and tokens. ("To a superstitious eye," writes Scott, "Lucy Ashton . . . might have suggested the idea of the murdered Nymph of the Fountain.") But in his pledge to Lucy, Edgar has violated another oath: "In the evening which succeeded my poor father's funeral, I cut a lock from my hair, and, as it consumed in the fire, I swore that my rage and revenge should pursue his enemies, until they shrivelled up before me like that scorched-up symbol of annihilation." That oath he now acknowledges to have been a "deadly sin," yet in the end it is carried out and the Ashton family does indeed shrivel before him or because of him. And Edgar acts knowingly, foreseeing that "there is a fate upon me, and I must go, or I shall add the ruin of others to my own," but defying, or inviting, that fate.

Still another omen shadows their leaving. As they rise, an arrow shot by Lucy's younger brother whistles through the air and strikes a raven, seated on the branch of a nearby oak: "The bird fluttered a few yards and dropped at the feet of Lucy, whose dress was stained with some spots of its blood," as her dress will be when she stabs her bridegroom in the bridal chamber.

Ravenswood passes by the Mermaiden's Fountain again, after he has been turned out of Ravenswood Castle by Lady Ashton. There he sees a vision—not of Lucy, as he first believes, but of old Alice, sitting on the grass. He is puzzled, she is blind and decrepit and can hardly leave her cottage. Her lips move but she does not speak, and as he advances she "moved or glided backward" and disappears among the trees. Riding on to Alice's cottage, he finds her lying dead on her pallet. The vision, then, must either have been of her specter come to give him warning, or have been a hallucination, the product of his deeply disturbed mind—yet Ravenswood's horse was "sweating and terrified."

Like *Macbeth*, *The Bride of Lammermoor* has its witches, a comparison suggested by Scott—three ancient hags, headed by the fearsome Ailsie Gourlay. Less powerful than Shakespeare's witches, although quite as malevolent, they function primarily as a chorus, commenting on the action and predicting doom. Scott, the rationalist, denies that they have supernatural powers, though admitting that they sometimes played the part, exploiting the fears and superstitions of the people even at risk of the "red gown"—death by fire, the stake, and the tar barrel. Ailsie denies that she has ever met the devil, "the foul thief," though she has "dreamed of him many a time"—yet she can foretell the future with uncanny accuracy.

Their malice seems aimed less at any individual than at life itself. They first appear to prepare old Alice for burial, taking a ghoulish pleasure in their work, and one of them gives another disillusioning glimpse of the Ravenswood past: "I mind when the father of this Master of Ravenswood that is now standing before us sticked young Blackhall with his whinger, for a wrang word said ower their wine . . . he gaed in as light as a lark, and he came out wi' his feet foremost. I was at the winding of the corpse; and when the bluid was washed off, he was a bonny bouk [bulk] of man's body." Ailsie prophecies as well, predicting that young Ravenswood will never be stretched out for burial, and that neither will he die in battle—"he'll no be graced sae far." Her knowledge, she adds, comes "frae a hand sure eneugh."

Watching the bridal procession to the church, Ailsie mutters her warning: "D'ye see yon dandilly maiden, a' glistenin' wi' gowd and jewels . . . . Her sand has but few grains to rin out." The wedding feast itself is marked by an ill omen. As Lady Ashton prepares to open the dancing with the groom, she suddenly notices that the family portraits on the wall have been altered, and that Sir William's father has been replaced by old Sir Malise Ravenswood, who "seemed to frown wrath and vengeance upon the party assembled below." And at Lucy's burial, the hags gather again, gloating over misfortune: "can a' the dainties they could gie us be half sae sweet as this hour's vengeance? There they are that were capering on their prancing nags four days since, and they are now ganging as dreigh and sober as oursells the day. They were a' glistening wi' gowd and silver; they're now as black as the crook [a chain holding a cooking pot over the fireplace]. And Miss Lucy Ashton, that grudged when an honest woman came near her—a taid [toad]may sit on her coffin the day, and she can never scunner [shudder] when he croaks."

And Ailsie knows—has somehow arranged it?—how the picture of Sir Malise came to be hanging on the wall. And it is Ailsie who gleefully notes that there is a thirteenth (Ravenswood) among the muffled pallbearers, and that "if auld freits [omens] say true, there's ane o' that company that'll no be lang for this warld." "That gude will come of it, nane of them need ever think to see," says Ailsie, and death comes of it when Colonel Ashton, Lucy's older brother, recognizes his enemy and angrily challenges him to a duel to the death, without witnesses, at dawn the next day. With the Master's death in a quicksand, as he rides to meet Colonel Ashton, the Ravenswood line comes to its end, while "The family of Ashton did not long survive that of Ravenswood."

These signs and warnings, bordering on the supernatural, may not directly determine the action of *The Bride of Lammermoor*, but they are essential to it. They influence the characters, Ravenswood above all but the impressionable Lucy as well, and they influence the reader. This sense of inevitability, of watching a doom-laden action unfold, contributes essentially to the emotional effect of the work, magnifying the importance of its characters and events, creating the tragic emotions of pity and fear.

Only five or six years after Scott's death, Gaetano Donizetti composed *Lucia di Lammermoor*, the most successful of all the many operatic versions of Scott novels (*Lucia* today may have more listeners than the *The Bride of Lammermoor* has readers). To be turned into an opera libretto, a novel must be drastically condensed, almost to the point of unrecognizability at times. *Lucia* keeps only what Donizetti and his librettist considered essential—the story of the two lovers belonging to hostile families, with its shocking outcome. Most of Scott's characters disappear—Lucy's family, for example, is reduced to a tyrannical brother. So, likewise, disappears everything distinctively Scottish. All sense of historical background vanishes, and with it nearly all of the signs and prophecies. The setting is simply the generalized place-time of grand opera.

As its title indicates, the opera, unlike the novel, centers on Lucy. With the celebrated mad scene as its climax, Donizetti's music communicates the depth and pathos of Lucy's love more powerfully than Scott's prose can do. Shakespeare's poetry might have been equal to the task, but Lucy's elaborate, polysyllabic sentences are not: "'And why do you now,' said Lucy, 'recall sentiments so terrible—sentiments so inconsistent with those you profess for me—with those your importunity has prevailed on me to acknowledge?'" Scots, not English, is the language of feeling in the Waverley Novels. Historically, a girl of Lucy's age and background would surely have spoken Scots, but regardless of history, a Scott heroine *must* speak proper English. Lucy can break that barrier only in her madness, in her final, derisive speech: "So, you have ta'en up your bonny bridegroom?"

What *The Bride of Lammermoor* gains, with its length and its slower movement, is the rich detail, the dense fictional world inhabited by its characters, and the resulting sense of a tragic fate hanging over them, all this giving them more than individual significance. Living in different worlds, Edgar and Lucy are drawn together by the very differences that make their union impossible, and that impossibility, sensed by readers from the outset, creates the deepest emotional effect of any of the Waverley Novels.

Chapter Ten

Ivanhoe

Scott's productivity was nearly incredible—as though the author of the Waverley Novels had been a syndicate rather than a man: "December 1819 saw the completion of *Ivanhoe*—March 20 of *The Monastery*, *The Abbot* in September, and *Kenilworth* in the January following."[1] But the public had not yet tired of its favorite. The first edition of ten thousand copies, at thirty shillings a copy (a week's wage for a skilled workman), promptly sold out. Here was a Waverley Novel set in England instead of Scotland, in the twelfth century instead of the comparatively recent past. Patriotic readers welcomed this turn to their own history and the novel's theme of national unity, and were thrilled as well by the siege of Torquilstone Castle, fascinated by Rebecca, the lovely Jewess, and moved by the pathos of her hopeless passion for Ivanhoe. Reviewers were equally delighted. "A splendid masque," said the *Quarterly Review*; "a splendid Poem," said the *Edinburgh Review*; "never was the illusion of fancy so complete," observed *Blackwood's*.[2]

Ivanhoe added to Scott's European fame as well. Visiting Paris in 1826, he saw an operatic version, richly produced, at the Comédie française. The great Goethe, after reading *Ivanhoe*, pronounced that he discovered in Scott's work "a wholly new art which has its own laws."[3] Without the strangeness of Scottish dialect and the little-known details of Scottish history, the novel was more accessible to European readers (chivalry and the church were parts of their heritage as well), and its rather formal standard English was easily translatable.

Ivanhoe seemed new, yet familiar—almost a guarantee of popularity. As in *Waverley* there are two heroines—the blonde and proper Rowena and the dark, intense Rebecca. Again, the hero—Wilfred of Ivanhoe—has been dispossessed, disinherited by his father, Cedric, who is angered by his son's friendship with King Richard I, the famous Coeur de Lion (Lion-Heart) and by his love for Rowena. Cedric, a fanatical Saxon nationalist, hates the ruling Normans and hopes to revitalize the Saxon cause by marrying Rowena, a descendant of King Alfred, to Athelstane, who is descended from Harold, the last Saxon king. Like the Jacobites of *Waverley* and *Rob Roy*, Cedric expects to reverse the verdict of history—and with no more success. Returning, penniless, from the Holy Land where he has been crusading with Richard, Ivanhoe enters a great tournament at Ashby-de-la-Zouche under the name of "El Desdichado," or "the Disinherited." His horse and armor are provided by Isaac, a rich Jew of York. Ivanhoe vanquishes all his opponents, including an old enemy, Brian de Bois-Guilbert, but is gravely wounded himself. Isaac's daughter, Rebecca, tends his wounds.

Passing through a forest after leaving Ashby, Isaac, Rebecca, Rowena, Ivanhoe, Cedric, and Athelstane are all captured by retainers of the ferocious Front-de-Boeuf (literally "Bull's-brow") and imprisoned in his castle of Torquilstone. The kidnapping is a collaboration: Front-de-Boeuf means to torture Isaac for ransom; Maurice de Bracy, a mercenary captain, expects to marry Rowena for her fortune; and Bois-Guilbert has been infatuated by Rebecca and intends to make her his mistress, even though he is a Knight Templar, a military monk sworn to chastity. But the prisoners are saved when the outlaws of Robin Hood and the oppressed peasants of the neighborhood storm the castle, directed by Richard himself, who has secretly returned from his Crusade. Front-de-Boeuf dies, de Bracy is captured, and Bois-Guilbert escapes with Rebecca. Saxons, led by a Norman, fighting Norman oppressors —here, the novel seems to imply, is a foreshadowing of the future unity, a nation not of Saxons, as Cedric hopes, but of Englishmen.

Bois-Guilbert has violated his vows, but when his act is discovered, the Grand Master of the Templars decides that Rebecca must have bewitched him. She is convicted of sorcery and sentenced to death by fire, but claims the right to trial by combat—if anyone can be found to fight for a Jew. Ivanhoe, still weak from his wound, appears at the last moment to defend Rebecca; Bois-Guilbert, who loves Rebecca, can save himself only by fighting as her accuser. They meet, Ivanhoe is unhorsed, but the victorious Bois-Guilbert reels and falls dead from his saddle. (Torn between his passion for Rebecca and his need to save himself, he "dies of his own internal disorder," as one critic puts it.)[4] Richard retakes his throne from his treacherous brother, John; Cedric abandons his dream of a Saxon England and is reconciled to his son, a Normanized Saxon possessing the best qualities of both races; Ivanhoe and Rowena marry, while Rebecca and Isaac leave England, hoping to be treated with greater humanity in Moslem Spain. Ivanhoe has never quite realized her devotion to him, and in any case could not return it, although he will remember her from time to time.

In spite of its multitude of characters and intricate story line, the basic structure of *Ivanhoe* is diagrammatic in its simplicity. The book is organized around three great scenes—the tournament, the attack on Torquilstone, and the trial by combat. The central scene is the longest, the most important, and by far the most striking. The ideal of the Waverley Novels is an ordered society in which men of all ranks are protected by and obedient to the law. Torquilstone Castle, in contrast, is a place of horrors; its master an embodiment of feudal savagery, who holds absolute power within its walls, and is capable of any crime. (He is guilty of patricide, having killed his father in a drunken quarrel over the beautiful Saxon woman, Ulrica.) The ordeal of the captives opens with parallel scenes, in which Front-de-Boeuf, de Bracy, and Bois-Guilbert confront their victims and make their demands, but each interview is broken off at the climax, as a bugle-call sounds the alarm, interrupting their "plans of avarice and of license."

The attack follows immediately. Scott's presentation is indirect—Rebecca, stationed at a window, describes what she sees for Ivanhoe, who is still too weak to rise from his couch. Rebecca's ignorance of war, and her questions, reflect the ignorance of the reader, and her horror at the bloodshed she sees contrasts dramatically with Ivanhoe's growing excitement and frustration that he can take no part in such a noble action. She cannot see everything from her window, and her incomplete vision communicates the confusion of the battle and the uncertainty of the outcome.

Front-de-Boeuf, mortally wounded by Richard, is rescued by his men and carried off to a chamber, where he is burned to death as Ulrica, now a fiendish hag, torches the castle and taunts the dying man. That death is appropriate—Front-de-Boeuf had threatened to roast Isaac alive unless he paid an enormous ransom, and was about to commence the torture when interrupted by the attack. De Bracy, who has a touch of wild chivalry in his nature, fights Richard, is beaten, and is spared. Bois-Guilbert, the most dangerous of them, escapes from the burning castle, throwing Rebecca across his horse and riding through the attackers.

The Norman characters of the novel are Richard, Front-de-Boeuf, De Bracy and Bois-Guilbert, Prince John and his followers, and the fanatical Lucas de Beaumanoir, Grand Master of the Templars, who condemns Rebecca; the Saxons are Cedric, Ivanhoe, Wamba the Jester, Gurth the Swineherd, Robin Hood ("Locksley") and his men, including the jolly Friar Tuck (here called "the Clerk of Copmanhurst"); Isaac and Rebecca are the Jews. Normans and Saxons are still intensely aware of their identity, more than 130 years after the Norman Conquest. The Normans are oppressive rulers; the Saxons, with a few exceptions like Cedric and Athelstane, are resentful serfs. Saxons hate Normans, Normans despise Saxons. Jews, the outsiders, are hated and persecuted by both. But Scott's presentation has more to do with nineteenth-century stereotypes than with medieval realities. His Saxons are "typical" Englishmen, blunt, rough, but essentially good-natured;

his Normans are haughty Frenchmen, sometimes polite but likely to be cruel and treacherous. Jews, of course, are usurers.

The Saxons may have been crushed at Hastings, but Cedric, one of the few men of his race to possess wealth and power, hopes to use the confusion of the time to establish Athelstane as ruler of England. But Athelstane's nickname, the Unready (derived from Ethelred the Unready, a tenth-century Saxon king), predicts the failure of Cedric's hope and implies a Saxon quality—they were conquered because they were unready. Athelstane, in fact, embodies the Norman stereotype of the Saxon—a hulking body without brain or spirit, living only to drink and feed. Cedric, finally, is forced to give up his dream. The future of England, implies the novel, lies in the unification of the two races and cultures, blending the best of them both into a new creation, the Englishman. That blending has already been accomplished in Ivanhoe himself, and before the end of the novel Richard has come to learn the true value of his Saxon subjects—whom Prince John, the contemptible usurper, ignorantly despises.

The name under which Ivanhoe fights at Ashby, "the Disinherited," could have applied almost equally well to "Brown" in *Guy Mannering* or "Lovell" in *The Antiquary* or Morton in *Old Mortality*. But here it has more than a personal significance; Ivanhoe's race has been disinherited as well. Like Brown and Lovell, Ivanhoe finds a sort of foster father (King Richard) who aids him to regain his inheritance. Like Brown and Lovell again, Ivanhoe is active in the opening section of the novel—as if to establish his qualifications for the role of hero—and passive for the remainder, simply disappearing for long sections.

He is confronted by Bois-Guilbert, the principal villain, who at times seems almost heroic in his fantastic schemes to establish an empire in the East, with Rebecca as his queen, and in the daring freedom of his thought—his total contempt for superstition of every sort, including the Christianity that he has sworn to defend. Bois-Guilbert dies, as he must, but not at the hands of the hero—who, like the earlier Scott heroes, kills no one. To the medieval mind, and also to the nineteenth-century reader, his death signifies the injustice of his cause. Naturalistically, it can be interpreted as the consequence of the struggle between his passion for Rebecca and the role he is forced to play to protect himself.

Of the other fictional characters, Front-de-Boeuf is surely the most striking—a monstrous figure, monstrous in his size and strength, in his appetites, in his brutality, and in his uncontrolled power—typifying the lawless savagery of his age, the reality that contrasts so bitterly with the ideal of chivalry. Although a nobleman and a knight, he, not "Locksley," is the true outlaw—the man whose desires are his only rule. The portrayal of Front-de-Boeuf, and the entire Torquilstone section, demonstrate that Scott is no uncritical glorifier of the Middle Ages or of feudalism. Wamba the Jester and Gurth the swineherd, and Locksley the "outlaw," in contrast, stand for the Saxon people—Wamba with his fidelity and courage, Gurth with his stubborn desire for freedom, and Locksley, or Robin Hood, with his unyielding resistance to injustice and oppression.

Above all, Rebecca fascinated readers of the early nineteenth century. Scott's treatment of his Jewish characters, Isaac and Rebecca, and of anti-Semitism is of course conditioned by his own time, when legal disabilities against Jews still survived (Jews could not sit in Parliament until some forty years later), and traditional stereotypes were strong. Isaac, Rebecca's father, is simply the Jewish usurer, equally contemptible for his cowardice and his avarice, although somewhat humanized by his love for his daughter. He is a milder Shylock, without the passion for revenge that gives Shylock dignity. But Scott, unlike Shakespeare, intermittently reminds us that Isaac's greed and his cowardice are both historically conditioned rather than inherent qualities of the Jew. The odious role of usurer was forced on the Jew by Christians, who then condemned him for taking it, and he is the constant victim of persecution against which he can defend himself only with his money.

Rebecca, too, is a stereotype, though to lesser degree—the Jew's daughter who falls in love with a Christian, like Jessica in *The Merchant of Venice*, or Abigail in Marlowe's *Jew of Malta*. But they are converted, while Rebecca remains a Jew. Male readers fell in love with her, female readers identified with her. Reviewers praised her ecstatically: "by far the most romantic creation of female character the author has ever formed—and second, we suspect, to no creature of female character whatever that is to be found in the whole annals either of poetry or of romance," said *Blackwoods*.[5] They admired Rebecca's courage, her beauty, her skill in healing, and her humanity (shown in her readiness to heal her persecutors), and they pitied her unreturned devotion to Ivanhoe.

Like *Waverley*, *Ivanhoe* is a novel with two heroines—a blonde heroine and a brunette, the dark heroine more passionate, more intelligent, and, at least potentially, more voluptuous than the blonde. In his initial description of Rebecca, as she sits in the stands of the tournament at Ashby, Scott draws attention to her bosom in a way that he would never have done with any of his blonde heroines: "the profusion of her sable tresses . . . fell down upon as much of a lovely neck and bosom as a simarre of the richest Persian silk . . . permitted to be visible . . . of the golden and pearl-studded clasps which closed her vest from the throat to the waist, the three uppermost were left unfastened on account of the heat, which something enlarged the prospect to which we allude."

The difference between the heroines is strikingly dramatized in their behavior during their captivity at Torquilstone. When de Bracy comes to woo Rowena, she proudly rejects him, until she learns that Ivanhoe also is a prisoner, then collapses in tears, embarrassing and confusing de Bracy. But when Bois-Guilbert goes to Rebecca in the high chamber where she is imprisoned and tells her that her only alternative to instant rape is to accept Christianity and "go forth in such state that many a Norman lady shall yield" to her in pomp and beauty, Rebecca throws open a latticed window, stands on the edge of the parapet, and threatens to throw herself down the instant he moves toward her. "Her high and firm resolve, which corresponded so well with the expressive beauty of her countenance, gave to her looks, air, and manner a dignity that aseemed more than mortal"—simultaneously forcing Bois-Guilbert to swear that he will do her no violence, and causing him to fall more deeply in love with her.

Readers could pity Rebecca for the love that she can never express and admire her courage—no doubt simultaneously admiring their own freedom from prejudice. But for a Jew to love a Christian is forbidden. "There is a gulf betwixt us. Our breeding, our faith, alike forbid either to pass over it," says Rebecca, and she must pay for her forbidden love by going into exile for the rest of her life, devoting her thoughts to Heaven and her actions to tending the sick and feeding the hungry, as if she were a sort of Jewish nun. What might be her consolation, she can never know—that "it would be inquiring too curiously to ask whether the recollection of Rebecca's beauty and magnanimity did not recur to his [Ivanhoe's] mind more frequently than the fair descendant of Alfred might altogether have approved."

If the author had allowed Ivanhoe to return Rebecca's love, which he does not, one solution was obvious and available—let Rebecca be baptized, and marriage with a Christian would be permitted, as it had been for Shylock's daughter. But that solution would destroy the characterization, and when it is offered to her (by Rowena, ironically, who is ignorant of Rebecca's devotion to Ivanhoe), she refuses: "I may not change the faith of my fathers like a garment unsuited to the climate in which I seek to dwell." Rebecca's faith—and this is a striking novelty—is treated throughout with deep respect.

Ivanhoe is, in effect, an antiromantic romance, simultaneously indicting the brutality of the age it presents, while exploiting its picturesque possibilities. That dual approach is clearest perhaps in the description of the tournament, with its pageantry and excitement, and with the reader's admiration for the prowess of the unknown knight, "El Desdichado," and his chivalrous behavior both in single combats and in the general melee at the finish. But admiration is promptly undercut by authorial irony: "Thus ended the memorable field of Ashby-de-la-Zouche, one of the most gallantly contested tournaments of that age; for although only four knights, including one who was smothered by the heat of his armour, had died upon the field, yet upward of thirty were desperately wounded, four or five of whom never recovered. Several more were disabled for life; and those who escaped best carried the marks of the conflict to the grave with them. Hence it is always mentioned in the old records as the 'gentle and joyous passage of arms of Ashby.'"

In fact, only two characters in the novel, Ivanhoe and Richard, actually live by the chivalric code. De Bracy, Front-de-Boeuf, Bois-Guilbert, Prince John and his supporters—all are motivated by greed, or fear, or lust, whether for power or for beauty. And while Scott's presentation of Richard is sympathetic, the verdict on his career—his performance of his role as king, as distinct from his personality—is severe: "the wild spirit of chivalry" leads him to pursue "the brilliant but useless career of a knight of romance," while ignoring his royal duties. His "feats of chivalry" might provide material for minstrels to celebrate, but his reign conferred no "solid benefits" upon his country. And Scott surely expected some of his readers to remember that within a few years of his return, Richard would be killed, uselessly, while besieging a minor castle in France.

The appeal of chivalry to the imagination is strong, and it gets full acknowledgment in the debate between Rebecca and Ivanhoe, as she describes the attack on Torquilstone to him (herself forced to admire the deeds of the unknown Black Knight, who is in fact Richard). Ivanhoe laments his weakness and protests that he would gladly "endure ten years' captivity to fight one day by that good knight's side in such a quarrel as this." Almost a formal debate follows. "The love of battle is the food upon which we live—the dust of the *melee* is the breath of our nostrils," exclaims Ivanhoe, when Rebecca tells him that his excitement may delay his recovery.

What is chivalry but "vain glory?," asks Rebecca. What remains of all the bloodshed, of all the suffering endured and inflicted, at the end of life? "Glory!," is Ivanhoe's answer again. And Rebecca realistically defines "glory": it is the rusted armor over a tomb, "the defaced sculpture of the inscription," it is the "rude rhymes" of a wandering minstrel. Ivanhoe's answer defends the ideal of chivalry—it alone "distinguishes the noble from the base," the knight from the "churl and the savage," it is "the stay of the oppressed, the redresser of grievances," it curbs the power of the tyrant. Rebecca yields, outwardly: until God raises up a new champion for his chosen people, "it ill beseemeth the Jewish damsel to speak of battle or of war."

But she has had the best of the argument, and all of the Waverley Novels, with their ideal of moderation and lawful order, are on her side. In any case, the circumstances argue more strongly than words. She and Ivanhoe are prisoners in the castle of Front-de-Boeuf, a knight, but more savage than any "churl"; she has barely escaped rape by another knight, and a third has attempted to force Rowena into marriage. And Bois-Guilbert, at least, loves glory and "honor" as much as Ivanhoe or Richard. *Ivanhoe* acknowledges the glamour of the chivalric ideal, while enforcing realization of the gap between it and reality. Nowhere is chivalry shown to be an effectual defense of the weak against the strong, a bulwark against the disorder and the cruelty of the age.

Ivanhoe shows no more sympathy toward the Catholic church. Christianity, as taught and practiced by the church, seems to do no more than chivalry to soften the manners and behavior of the period. Besides the Clerk of Copmanhurst, whose "clerkship" is mostly a joke, organized Christianity is represented principally by two hypocrites and a bigot, by Prior Aymer, who lives for sexual pleasure, and Bois-Guilbert, the atheist Templar who freely violates his vows, and on the other hand by the merciless Grand Master of the Templars, Lucas de Beaumanoir.

It may seem ironic, then, that Scott should have been blamed in his own time as a reactionary who wished to revive the evils and oppression of the past, or that enthusiastic admirers of *Ivanhoe* staged absurd mock tournaments. "The old world is to him a crowded map; the new one a dull, hateful blank," wrote one contemporary (who nevertheless admired the Waverley Novels). "He dotes on all well-authenticated superstitions; he shudders at the shadow of innovation."[6]

Two generations later, Mark Twain, in his *Life on the Mississippi*, echoed that condemnation, blaming Scott's influence for everything he disliked in Southern culture—"the duel, the inflated speech, and the jejune romanticism of an inflated past." Scott had "checked the wave of progress," he had "run the people mad . . . with his inflated romances," and the influence of his work was responsible for the building of sham castles, for the "windy humbuggeries" of Southern prose, and for the Southern cult of violence (product of a false sense of "honor"). Scott might even be held responsible for the Civil War, he "had so large a hand in making Southern character." (The full indictment can be found in chapters 40, "Castles and Culture," and 46, "Enchantments and Enchanters," of *Life on the Mississippi*.) Twain's own *A Connecticut Yankee in King Arthur's Court*, with its ruthless burlesque of "chivalry," can easily be read as an intended corrective. In seeing *Ivanhoe* as an unqualified glorification of the Middle Ages in all their aspects, Mark Twain appears to have misread *Ivanhoe*—a creative misreading, certainly. But that misreading is hardly surprising. Scott is deeply aware of brutality and oppression, yet fascinated by the Robin Hood and Richard the Lion-Heart of legend, exploiting the "romantic" possibilities of his period, and even seeing it as decisive in the making of the modern Englishman.

In fact, *Ivanhoe* is deeply unhistorical. Scott's Protestant prejudices prevented him from understanding the central role of the Catholic church in the medieval world, and his assumption of a conscious and deep-seated hostility between Norman and Saxon, a hundred and thirty years after the Norman Conquest, seems to have no basis in history. The nineteenth century was deeply conscious of nationality, of race, and of language—a consciousness increased by the influence of Scott's novels. The twelfth century was conscious, above all, of rank and class. If the nobles of England despised and oppressed their serfs, it was because they were serfs, not because they were Saxons, and the monkish chroniclers of the time bitterly condemned the cruelty of the nobles but never denounced them as oppressive foreigners.

Scott builds his novel around a contrast between Norman and Saxon, as he had built earlier novels around contrasts between Highland and Lowland, Jacobite and Hanoverian, Covenanter and Royalist. But those contrasts, firmly based on historical reality, could be made richly circumstantial. Lacking that basis, *Ivanhoe*'s contrast between Norman and Saxon is vague and stereotyped: "the vanquished distinguished by their plain, homely, blunt manners, and the free spirit infused by their ancient institutions and laws; the victors, by the high spirit of military fame, personal adventure, and whatever could distinguish them as the flower of chivalry." Oppression of the people is referred to, but almost never shown, and the only serfs who actually appear—Wamba and Gurth—are in fact the serfs of a Saxon landlord, Cedric.

The world of *Ivanhoe* seems barer, more sparsely furnished, and less varied in its human types, than the world of *Guy Mannering* or *Old Mortality*. And this impression is not simply a result of the simpler society that is presented in *Ivanhoe*—a society that in historical fact must have been richly diversified. Scott could not know enough about the "manners" of that remote time to present them as fully and as convincingly as he had presented the manners of late seventeenth-century Scotland in *Old Mortality*. The grit of reality is missing—the hunger, the cold, the stinks, the sheer discomfort that medieval life must have continuously inflicted. And, somehow, there is no real suffering. At the attack on Torquilstone, men are killed and horribly wounded, yet no one actually seems to be *hurt*.

Language offered a formidable obstacle to historical realism. Scott's Normans would have spoken a form of French, his Saxons of English—both unintelligible to modern readers. Since authenticity is impossible, Scott arrives at the inevitable compromise; the language of his characters, he writes in his introduction to the 1830 edition, "should admit, if possible, no word or turn of phraseology betraying an origin directly modern."

But that rule seems impossible to follow. When Rebecca speaks to Rowena—"'Farewell,' she said. 'May He who made both Jew and Christian shower down on you His choicest blessings! The bark that wafts us hence will be under weigh ere we can reach the port'"—the modern reader easily recognizes that this is the speech of a woman of the early nineteenth century, not of the twelfth. Or, to be exact, that it is the speech of a heroine in a novel of the early nineteenth century. No writer can purge his language of all the peculiarities of his own time, not only of the words that would not have been spoken earlier, but of the sentiments that would not have been thought. Perhaps the past can never be seen as it *really* was; it can only be viewed from the standpoint of whatever present the writer or the reader may inhabit. Only intimate knowledge of the period chosen can reduce—but never eliminate—the resulting anachronisms. Inevitably, then, *Ivanhoe* incorporates not only the language but the ideology—the racial, sexual, and historical myths and stereotypes—of the early nineteenth century.

But few readers of Scott's own day, whether English, European, or American, raised objections. His experiment had been a success, and the whole world of European history, at least since the early Middle Ages, seemed to be open to him.

Chapter Eleven
The Waverley Novels—
Their Place in Literature

With *The Bride of Lammermoor*, the series of novels set in the Scotland of the preceding 150 years comes to an end, and with it Scott's most significant contribution to the English novel. He searched constantly for novelty of setting—the Protestant Reformation in Scotland in *The Monastery* (1820) and *The Abbot* (1820); Elizabethan England in *Kenilworth* (1820), in which the great queen herself appears; Jacobean England in *The Fortunes of Nigel* (1822), notable for its comic yet sympathetic portrayal of James I; the England of Charles II and the Popish Plot in *Peveril of the Peak* (1822); fifteenth-century France during the quarrels between Louis XI and Charles the Bold, duke of Burgundy, in *Quentin Durward* (1823), a book that greatly advanced Scott's European reputation; *St. Ronan's Well* (1824), a satirical portrayal of "manners" at a semifashionable resort in contemporary Scotland; twelfth-century Wales in *The Betrothed* (1825); Richard the Lion-Heart's crusade in *The Talisman* (1825); Cromwell's England in *Woodstock* (1826); medieval Scotland in *The Fair Maid of Perth* (1828), in which the hero is drawn for once from the middle class, and displays a striking bourgeois vigor; Switzerland's war for independence against Charles the Bold in *Anne of Geierstein* (1829); the Byzantine Empire at the time of the first Crusade in *Count Robert of Paris* (1831); and Scotland's struggle for freedom under Robert the Bruce in *Castle Dangerous* (1831).

Nearly all of these books contain striking characters and scenes, but discriminating readers, including the author, recognized a gradual decline. Only when he returned to his favorite scene and period, as in *Redgauntlet*, or the short story "The Two Drovers," did his work reach its former level. The principal journals stopped reviewing the Waverley Novels as they appeared, taking them up two or three at a time rather than individually, or ignoring them entirely. But his British audience continued to grow, as the earlier novels began to come out in cheap editions, and the European audience widened enormously as translations of his works appeared. There can be no doubt that from 1815 to 1830, at least, Scott was the most widely read novelist in the world.

Heroes and Heroines

Surveying the Waverley Novels as a whole, one is struck by the continuity displayed in these twenty-three novels written over a period of about sixteen years. Certainly Scott chooses new scenes, new periods, even writes a tragic *Bride of Lammermoor*, but his themes, his conflicts, and his character types inevitably tend to repeat themselves. "How uniformly Scott fails in his attempt at imaginative characters!,"[1] Coleridge exclaimed. "They are all alike from Meg Merrilies to Norna." Clearly there are strong similarities, particularly among Meg Merrilies in *Guy Mannering*, Norna of the Fitful Head in *The Pirate*, Edie Ochiltree in *The Antiquary*, Wandering Willie in *Redgauntlet*—all powerful, aged figures, masters of language and of lore, often speaking in riddles and rhymes, guardians of tradition and embodiments of folk culture. Only by trusting them and submitting to their guidance can the heroes succeed—as though the land itself, or rather its culture, is accepting them.

The bores and pedants are much alike throughout the novels. We find also the "Dandie Dinmont type"—the rough, honest, kind-hearted farmer—and the shrewd, sometimes rascally servant who is contrasted with his impractical master—Cuddie Headrigg in *Old Mortality* and Andrew Fairservice in *Rob Roy*. But the most striking repetition is the sameness of the heroes and heroines. There are only two notable exceptions: *The Heart of Midlothian*, in which the stock heroine does not appear at all and the stock hero (Reuben Butler) has a minor role; and *The Fair Maid of Perth*, in which the hero, Henry Wynd, for once is drawn from the middle class instead of the aristocracy, and displays a bourgeois energy lacking in his counterparts.

Readers and critics have always found the official heroes and heroines to be the least interesting characters of the Waverley Novels. From the vagueness with which most of them are described, it seems clear that Scott had never really imagined them; indeed, almost any pair would serve in almost any novel. The descriptions of Lovel and of Isabella Wardour in *The Antiquary* could apply to them all: the hero is "a young man of genteel appearance" and the heroine is of "tall and elegant figure" (alternatively, she may possess a "fairy form"). Except for Diana Vernon in *Rob Roy*, the heroine is blonde, and Scott's formula for Rowena in *Ivanhoe* could apply to them all: "her disposition was naturally that which physiognomists consider as proper to fair complexions—mild, timid, and gentle."

But Scott's heroines generally have only a minor part in the action of his novels, and consequently criticism has centered on the hero. He is essentially passive, "a thing never acting but perpetually acted upon," as Scott himself observed in *The Fortunes of Nigel* (although he may perform some dramatic action early in the novel, as if to establish his credentials). Like Lovel in *The Antiquary*, he asks nothing of society but "the privilege of walking innoxiously through the path of life, without jostling others or permitting myself to be jostled." John Leycester Adolphus, in his *Letters to Richard Heber* (1822), was the first critic to consider this quality of the hero at length.

"It has frequently been noticed as a fault," writes Adolphus, "that the hero . . . is not sufficiently important, and fails to maintain his legitimate pre-eminence above the other characters. One circumstance very common . . . and highly disadvantageous to the principal personage, is that during a great part of the story, he is made the blind or involuntary instrument of another's purposes, the attendant on another's will, and the sport of events over which he exercises no control." Thus the character of Frank Osbaldistone, in *Rob Roy*, lacks the "commanding interest which should surround the first personage of a novel" because he is constantly "played upon as a dupe, disposed of as a captive, tutored as a novice." Adolphus adds that "It is also the misfortune of many heroes in these works to be constantly thrown into shade by some more prominent character,"[2] as Waverley is by Fergus Mac-Ivor, Frank Osbaldistone by Rob Roy, Morton by Claverhouse and Burley, Ivanhoe by King Richard.

A modern critic, Alexander Welsh, has pointed out the curious fact that, with only one or two exceptions, the Scott hero never kills anyone. These are novels of adventure, the heroes are gentlemen trained in the use of weapons and expected to defend their honor, and the action commonly occurs in times and places characterized by violence, lawlessness, and often by rebellion or civil war. Yet Waverley's only concern at the Battle of Preston-pans seems to be to rescue enemy officers; Morton is a spectator at the Battle of Drumclog, and although he fights at the head of his men at Bothwell Bridge, we are simply told that he "fought"—the vaguest possible verb—not whether he succeeded in wounding or killing a single enemy; Ivanhoe is not allowed to kill his mortal enemy, Brian de Bois-Guilbert, who is instead struck down almost miraculously, "a victim of his own contending passions." That Scott could describe bloody action when he chose, he shows clearly enough in *Old Mortality*. When Burley kills Sergeant Bothwell, "with a laugh of savage joy," he "flourished his sword aloft, and then passed it through his adversary's body." But the hero invariably belongs to a new, more humane and enlightened age, an age when law is replacing unrestrained force; he cannot be allowed to participate in the violence of the past.

Adolphus notes that the hero is often absent, or only a spectator, at some crucial scene: thus Waverley "sinks into absolute insignificance, by sustaining only the part of a common spectator in the highly tragic scene of Mac-Ivor's and Evan Dhu's condemnation."[3] A similar example occurs in *Old Mortality* when Morton, already sure of his own pardon, watches the torture of Macbriar after the defeat of the Cameronians at Bothwell Bridge. Again, the hero often disappears from his novel for long periods, like Ivanhoe or Lovel or Brown-Bertram. The pattern can already be seen in the narrative poems. There, too, we find the passive hero, and in "The Lady of the Lake," Malcolm Graeme, the official hero, "continues in retirement till we hardly wish for his return."[4] This passivity of the hero is mental and emotional as well as physical; he may be supposed to experience struggles of conscience at times, but these internal conflicts are not actually presented.

As one reviewer noted, Scott's novels often contained both "a virtuous passive hero, who is to marry the heroine" and "a fierce active hero, who is to die a violent death, generally by hanging or shooting."[5] Such characters, the "dark heroes," include Fergus Mac-Ivor, Rob Roy, George Staunton, Redgauntlet, Cleveland the Pirate, even Bois-Guilbert, among others from the novels, Roderick Dhu (in *The Lady of the Lake*) and Marmion in the poems. The dark hero is a mixture of good and evil; he lives by passion, impulse, and desire rather than by adherence to the law and to the code of a gentleman. He acts and feels; he is the center of interest whenever he appears. The type is strongly Byronic, but represents an independent development; Marmion is a Byronic hero before Byron.

A "dark heroine" is also to be found in several of the novels—Effie Deans, for example, or Rebecca, or Diana Vernon. She is often more voluptuous in figure than the blonde, and she possesses a forcefulness, an emotional intensity, and often a wit and intelligence that are lacking in the official heroine. Such characters seemed morally ambiguous to Scott, even—paradoxically—unwomanly; like the dark heroes, they appeared to threaten the established moral code, based on submissiveness, self-denial, and restraint, and so to threaten the existence of society. Consequently, then, the dark heroines are likely to be dispatched to a convent or at least (like Rebecca) to a state of lifelong spinsterhood. Even Diana Vernon, who marries Frank Osbaldiston, is only a partial exception. When Frank tells his story, Diana is dead—a penalty, perhaps, for her unwomanly boldness. Flora Mac-Ivor seems a variation on the type; she is blonde, not dark, and her fanatical devotion to the Jacobite cause leaves no room for love, but she too is far more intelligent and forceful than the hero or the official heroine, and she too pays a high price for exercising these "unwomanly" qualities— "unwomanly," of course, by literary convention.

Scott himself, reviewing his own novels anonymously in the *Quarterly Review*, cited the weakness of the hero as one of their two principal failings (the

other being faulty plot construction). He explains this passivity by the fact
that his heroes were usually supposed to be strangers to Scotland, thus allowing the author to "enter into minute details, which are addressed to the reader
through the medium of the hero,"[6] and thereby aiding the author's portrayal
of manners—an explanation that may hold for Waverley, for Frank
Osbaldistone in *Rob Roy*, for Brown-Bertram and Lovel in *Guy Mannering*
and *The Antiquary*, but not for Henry Morton in *Old Mortality* or Edgar
Ravenswood in *The Bride of Lammermoor*. But this explanation seems a rationalization, and in any case will not hold for many of the Waverley Novels.
Scott recognized that "if he [the author] gains this advantage, it is by sacrificing the character of the hero. No one can be interesting to the reader who is
not, himself, a prime agent in the scene."

William Hazlitt, in an essay on "The Heroes of Romance" (1825), offers a
generic explanation; the sort of novel (or "romance," to use Hazlitt's term)
that Scott wrote, and the audience that he wrote for, required exactly the sort
of hero that he provided. The popular novelist cannot afford to give his protagonist any strikingly individual qualities, that might possibly cause of-
fense. The hero's character must be bland and wholesome, marked only by a
few good qualities that every reader is left free to improve upon as he or she
chooses, and if readers do not trouble themselves to fill in the blank, even that
is not fatal. As Scott's friend, Lady Louisa Stuart, observed, "the hero and the
heroine are the people one cares least about. But provided one does care
enough about somebody it is all one to me."[7]

Probing more deeply, George Lukács explains that Scott chose as protagonist a figure who "may, through character and fortune, enter into human contact with both sides,"[8] and so cannot be a fanatical partisan of either extreme.
That explanation clearly applies to Waverley and to Henry Morton, perhaps
also to Ivanhoe, and at least in part to Edgar Ravenswood, who makes such
an attempt and fails disastrously, but it does not describe the heroes of *Guy
Mannering* or *The Antiquary*—novels that deal with private life, which present no violently contending parties.

David Daiches has suggested that the true role of the Scott hero is to act as
a symbolic observer—a more sophisticated expression of Scott's own explanation. Such characters, says Daiches, cannot "step out of their symbolic roles
in order to act freely and provide that sense of abundant life which is so essential to a good novel." This sense of "abundant life," therefore, is "achieved by
the minor characters (and here again the comparison with Shakespeare suggests itself)."[9] The comparison is unconvincing; anyone thinking of
Shakespeare's major plays surely thinks first of the principal characters—of
Hamlet, not of Polonius, of Lear, not the Fool. A closer parallel can be found

in the Dickensian novel, where official heroes and heroines are also constrained by the requirements of gentility; *Nicholas Nickleby* may be entitled after its hero, but Mr. Squeers interests us a good deal more; readers of *Martin Chuzzlewit* will vividly recall Mrs. Gamp, but are likely to forget the name of Ruth Westlock, who marries Martin.

Language

Language matters. Novels are made of words, and clearly it is a serious weakness if an author's narrative style prevents the reader's close involvement in the action, if the dialogue prevents him from believing in the emotions the characters are described as feeling, and consequently in the characters themselves. But the Waverley Novels, at least the earlier ones, have two languages—English and Scots. The vernacular is used principally in dialogue; Scott employs it only once for extended narration, in "Wandering Willie's Tale" in *Redgauntlet*. The novels offer as well two significant subspecies of English. In *Old Mortality* and *The Heart of Midlothian* especially, there is a scriptural style, drawn from the English Bible, a style that is oral, popular, often figurative and deeply emotional. There is also the notorious "tushery"—"an echo chamber of Spenser and Chaucer and old balladeers and, loudest of all, Shakespeare's histories and comedies,"[10] as a recent critic describes it.

Examples enough have been quoted to suggest the wit, the liveliness, the freshness of imagery, the rhythm, and the emotional intensity of which Scott is capable when writing in his native dialect. His predicament is that of Burns, who complained about being compelled to write English poetry, because "I have not the command of the language that I have of my native tongue. . . . I think my ideas are more barren in English than in Scottish."[11] Writing in a stiff and conventional English, Burns was simply a minor versifier.

The linguistic situation Scott faced was entirely different from that confronted by any English novelist, even a regionalist like Thomas Hardy. Scots possessed a long and distinguished literary tradition and was still the general spoken language of the country; but broad Scots, at least, was rapidly disappearing from the speech of the educated. In a letter of 1822, Scott himself recorded the declining prestige of the vernacular speech: "Scotch was a language which we have heard spoken by the learned & the wise & witty . . . and which had not a trace of vulgarity in it, but on the contrary sounded rather graceful and genteel . . . it was different from the English as the Venetian from Tuscan dialect of Italy, but it never ocurd *sic* to anyone that the Scotish *sic* any more than the Venetian was more vulgar. . . . But that is all gone."

Well before the union of England and Scotland in 1707, Scots had gone out of use as a medium of serious prose. Its literary use in the eighteenth century was confined almost entirely to poetry—notably the poems of Burns. In the second half of the century, Edinburgh produced a brilliant intellectual life, but its writers used standard English and carefully avoided "Scotticisms." (There is a parallel in the conscious avoidance of "Americanisms" by American writers of the early nineteenth century.) David Hume, the greatest philosopher of the age, spoke broad Scots at home, but he would never have dreamed of writing philosophic dialogues in Scots. By the end of the century, the native speech had become a language under siege, a language reserved for popular speech and poetry.

Wishing to reach the widest possible audience, and bound by a demand for linguistic propriety (which he himself accepted), the Scottish writer found himself compelled to use what was essentially a foreign language, with all the difficulties that entailed. Some of those difficulties were described by Scott's friend, John Leyden. The Scotsman of the upper classes was "prohibited, by the imputation of vulgarity, from using the common language of the country, in which he expresses himself with most ease and vivacity, and clothed in which, his earliest and most distinct impressions always arise to his mind. He uses a species of translation, which checks the versatility of fancy, and restrains the genuine and spontaneous glow of his conceptions."[12] (The stiffness of Leyden's English illustrates his argument.) The need to make such a "species of translation" might fatally handicap the imaginative writer—Conrads and Nabokovs are extremely scarce. While eighteenth-century Scotland was capable of first-class work in philosophy, psychology, and history, its major achievement in "polite literature" (a term that excluded Burns) was John Home's mediocre tragedy, *Douglas* (1756).

A natural consequence of this linguistic situation was an extreme self-consciousness, with a resulting hypercorrectness and formality of style. "When an easy, idiomatical phrase occurs we dare not adopt it," wrote another of Scott's contemporaries. "We handle English, as a person who cannot fence handles a sword; continually afraid of hurting themselves with it . . . or making some awkward motion that shall betray our ignorance."[13] That explanation helps to account for the nature of Scott's narrative prose and of his upper-class dialogue. His own comment on Rob Roy's manner of speaking English, a "slow, pedantic mode of expression, arising from a desire to avoid peculiarities of idiom or dialect," characterizes his own style. Writing in Scots, or even in a lightly Scotticized English, freed him from that paralyzing need to be "genteel" and correct—but that Scots had always to be attributed to a character other than the hero or heroine, and never to the author himself. His heroes and heroines, required by literary convention to be ladies and gentlemen, avoid any imputation of vulgarity by speaking an excessively proper English, combining an abstract, polysyllabic vocabulary with an elaborate syntax. (Down to the end of the eighteenth century, Scottish ladies and gentlemen regularly spoke Scots at home—but they do not in the Waverley Novels. Linguistic propriety outweighed history.)

Examples of this peculiar diction can be found in abundance in any of the Waverley Novels; this one from a late work, *Castle Dangerous* (1831), is typical. The heroine is desperately trying to prevent a combat between two knights: "Think that this is Palm Sunday, and will you defile with blood such a peculiar festival of Christianity? Intermit your feud at least so far as to pass to the nearest church, bearing with you branches, not in the ostentatious mode of earthly conquerors, but as rendering due homage to the rulers of the blessed Church, and the institutions of our holy religion." The abstract diction and complicated syntax, carefully delaying the completion of meaning, cannot communicate the necessary sense of impending violence, or any feeling of anxiety; the language continuously draws attention to its own inappropriateness.

Our sense of inappropriateness increases when the style is extended to a lower-class character, like the illiterate gypsy Hayraddin Maugrabin, Quentin Durward's guide. "Where, then, is your boasted freedom?," asks Quentin, and Hayraddin replies: "In my thoughts, which no chains can bind; while yours, even when your limbs are free, remain fettered by your laws and your superstitions, your dreams of local attachment, and your fantastic visions of civil policy. . . ." Coleridge's comment seems justified: "Characterless or anti-characteristic as Scott's dialogues too commonly are, this is ultra-improbable, superlatively inappropriate."[14]

The speech of the heroes and heroines can be at least partly defended on grounds of historical realism as well as literary convention. Upper-class conversation may well have been more formal and ceremonious in the early nineteenth century than in the permissive twentieth. But it could never have approached the style of such passages. "Sir Walter always fails in well bred men and women—and yet who has seen more of both?"[15] remarked one contemporary. Neither can literary convention entirely account for such dialogue; Jane Austen's characters do not speak like this, and neither did Fielding's or Smollett's. The English of Scott's journal, in comparison, seems direct, concrete, almost colloquial. But the journal was private.

Scott's narrative prose shows the same qualities as his dialogue—often pretentious and diffuse, effectively distancing the action described, whether or not such distancing serves any purpose. It is a style that seems particularly unsuited for presenting physical action. Consider the death of Bois-Guilbert in *Ivanhoe*: "The trumpets sounded, and the knights charged each other in full career. The wearied horse of Ivanhoe and its no less exhausted rider, went down, as all had expected, before the well-aimed lance and vigorous steed of the Templar. This issue of the combat all had foreseen; but although the spear of Ivanhoe did but, in comparison, touch the shield of Bois-Guilbert, that champion, to the astonishment of all who beheld it, reeled in his saddle, lost his stirrups, and fell in the lists." The language is vague—Ivanhoe and his horse simply "went down." No more colorless words could be found. The passage is wordy—for example, the first clause of the third sentence is pure repetition—yet it is too brief; the details that would compel the reader to *see* are not there. To imagine the scene fully, we must create it for ourselves. Only in Scots, at least when writing for publication, could Walter Scott be direct, colloquial, concrete.

Composition and Technique

Scott's method of composition accounts for many of the distinctive qualities of his work. While it may not be literally true to say that he never revised, revision was strictly limited. At the end of each day's stint of writing, the manuscript would go off to the printers. There it would be recopied, usually by James Ballantyne (to prevent the printers from recognizing Scott's very distinctive hand), the text would be set in type from Ballantyne's copy, and the proofs would be annotated by Ballantyne and returned to the author, usually eight leaves at a time. Ballantyne did more than simply correct errors; he would question inconsistencies and make critical comments, and Scott took those comments seriously: "Passages were expanded at his direction, motivations became clearer, and large chunks of expository narrative were added."[16] Reading proof became part of the creative process.

Such a method naturally led to wordiness, but wordiness might be welcome if it helped to fill three or four volumes. Carlyle's acid comment on Lockhart's seven-volume life of Scott applies also to the Waverley Novels: "Seven volumes sell so much dearer than one; are so much easier to write," and one can hardly help agreeing with Carlyle's conclusion, that "There is a great discovery still to be made in Literature, that of paying literary men by the quantity they *do not* write."[17] Obviously, too, such a method made no allowance for afterthoughts, for changes of plan. If the young Guy Mannering practiced astrology in the early chapters, an action that would seem totally out of character as the novel developed and has no effect on the outcome, those early chapters had already been printed and they would stand. Not only was resetting type expensive, it would delay publication and the author would already have spent the expected profits.

Ordinarily Scott wrote with only the vaguest plan in his mind. (He probably spent more time and thought on laying out his plantations of trees at Abbotsford than on planning his novels.) He did not, could not, make elaborate outlines and scenarios. "I never could lay down a plan, or having laid it down, I never could adhere to it," he confesses in his journal (12 February 1826). "I only tried to make that which I was actually writing diverting and interesting, leaving the rest to fate." Characters became important or insignificant "according to the success with which I was able to bring them out." Two years later, again in his journal, he admits that he has no idea of how to bring *The Fair Maid of Perth* to a conclusion: "all my incidents and personages run into such a gordian knot of confusion to which I could devize no possible extrication."[18]

Experience had shown him that the solution would come, but not through conscious effort; often he had gone to bed after giving up the problem in frustration, and then "waked in the morning with a distinct and accurate conception of the mode . . . in which the plot might be extricated"[19]—particularly if he had taken an extra glass of wine the night before. In a sense, of course, the final outcome was always clear; the ending would be "happy" (except in *The Bride of Lammermoor*), meaning that the hero would marry the heroine and would come into property (land rather than money, to establish or confirm his status as a gentleman). There could be, of course, many ways of reaching this desired outcome; there might be either outright villains or "dark heroes" and occasionally heroines to complicate the action. Adult figures—father-substitutes—take the hero under their protection, as King Richard protects Ivanhoe, and he often finds guides and helpers among the common people.

Readers soon came to know what to expect. In discussing *The Fortunes of Nigel* (1822), the *Quarterly Review* neatly summarized the typical plot of the Waverley Novels: "The poor passive hero is buffeted about in the usual manner, involved, as usual, in the chicaneries of civil process, and exposed to the danger of a criminal execution, and rewarded by the hand of the heroine, such as she is, and the redemption of the mortgage on the family estate."[20] His social status is threatened, and his honor and/or loyalty cast in doubt by suspicious circumstances until he finally demonstrates that he is a gentleman, and therefore a thoroughly respectable and conventional member of society. The disinherited son in search of his heritage, the orphan in quest of his name, the outcast in search of his father—these time-honored situations are basic to the Waverley Novels.

As a maker of plots, Scott seems repetitive, careless, and awkward. His difficulties with beginnings and endings—the first often intolerably slow, the latter huddled and perfunctory—are obvious. A comment by David Daiches, usually a fervent admirer, on *Redgauntlet* can apply to many others of the Waverley Novels: Scott's greatest weakness in *Redgauntlet*, observes Daiches, is that he "uses the conventional plot patterns available to him to provide the external structure of his story, and these plot patterns are really quite unsuitable to the kind of exploration between tradition and progress which Scott is carrying out."[21]

The primary interest of a Scott novel, however, depends on its characterizations (principally of the "supporting" characters who in the prolonged absences of the hero often become the real protagonists) and on striking individual scenes. To many readers and reviewers, unity and coherence seemed unimportant if only the novelist told a good story. The *Edinburgh Review*, commenting on *The Fortunes of Nigel*, pointed out that the hero's "own scanty part . . . is performed in the vicinity of a number of other separate transactions," which were all thrown into a single work. "We should not care very much," the reviewer continues, "if this only destroyed the unity of the piece—but it sensibly weakens its interest and reduces it from the rank of a comprehensive and engaging narrative, in which every event gives and receives importance from its connexion with the rest, to that of a mere collection of sketches relating to the same period."[22] (Quite unintentionally, the reviewer demonstrates that far from being an irrelevant "artistic" consideration, unity creates interest.)

Scott and the Historical Novel

Paradoxically, the conservative Scott, who distrusted all "innovation" in politics and showed little interest in the radical literary experiments of the romantic poets, was himself an innovator, the inventor of a new genre or subgenre, the historical novel. (The popular Gothic novels might have had medieval settings, but they could not be called "historical" in any sense.) George Lukács suggests plausibly that the development of the form was conditioned by history, that the enormous political upheavals of the revolutionary and Napoleonic period must have indicated powerfully the direct and inescapable effect of history upon individual lives.

Only two or three of the Waverley Novels, and perhaps only one, avoid the historical classification—*St. Ronan's Well*, set in contemporary Scotland,

The Antiquary, located in the Scotland of the 1790s, and *Guy Mannering,* twenty years or more before *The Antiquary.* But in those two latter novels, Scott's primary interest seems to be in portraying "manners," character types, ways of life, that had vanished in his own more progressive era. (Victorian novelists, such as Dickens and George Eliot, learned from Scott the advantages of setting a novel a generation or so before the time of writing, and the detachment and perspective that could be gained.)

The closest literary analogue to the Waverley Novels was offered by Shakespeare's history plays, which Scott reread constantly, and he surely learned much from Shakespeare's readiness to mingle the humorous with the serious or tragic, to include Falstaff in the same play as Hotspur, or to bring Bardolph, Pistol and Fluellen into the martial world of the heroic Henry V. But there is an important difference. Shakespeare's attention is usually centered on the major historical figure, while in his earlier novels Scott treated such personages discreetly, introducing them briefly, if at all (the characters of *The Bride of Lammermoor,* for example, are all private persons, although at the same time they may be historical types), never allowing them to play central roles in the action.

Unlike Shakespeare's histories or Roman tragedies, a Waverley Novel is always constructed around a fictitious plot—perhaps to avoid the stereotyping likely to result from showing the major historical figure performing the actions for which he is celebrated. In general, "major figures" play a larger part in the later novels (Charles II and Cromwell both figure importantly in *Woodstock,* Louis XI and Charles the Bold, duke of Burgundy, in *Quentin Durward,* Richard Coeur de Lion and Saladin in *The Talisman*) and this development seems related to the comparative weakness of most of those works.

The sense of history in the earlier works, the "Scotch Novels," is not derived from a parade of historical figures across the pages, and usually not from a profusion of antiquarian detail or from an artificial "period" language. It results instead from the inseparable relationship of characters to their social, political, and economic backgrounds, so that one feels that Fergus Mac-Ivor, Rob Roy, or Sir William Ashton and Edgar Ravenswood could not have existed at any other moment of history. Usually, although not always, the sense of history depends also upon the involvement of the protagonist in the historical event, most commonly a violent crisis, a revolution, or a civil war (but never with an invasion: Scott's concern is with divided societies). Thus in *Old Mortality* one senses from the outset that no matter how strongly he may wish only to be left alone and to avoid taking a side, Morton cannot escape the history of his time; he must be drawn into the conflict of Royalists and rebellious Presbyterians.

For such writing, a profound knowledge of the past was needed, a knowledge that Scott had acquired through collecting ballads and folklore, and through endless reading of histories, memoirs, and old pamphlets. He was aware of the dangers of overwhelming the reader with his own accumulated knowledge of the past: the historical novelist, as he explained in his introduction to *Ivanhoe*, should not concentrate on the obsolete, but should emphasize "that extensive neutral ground . . . of manners and sentiments which are common to us and to our ancestors, having been handed down unaltered from them to us, or which, arising out of the principles of our common nature, must have existed alike in either state of society."

As might be expected, Scott was not greatly concerned about pedantic accuracy in minutiae, such as the date of a battle or details of a costume. He sought for parallels between present and past, and tried to discover the general trends beneath the conflicts on the surface of society. If he could achieve such insights, the occasional anachronism or error hardly mattered. He knew that history did not consist only of party conflicts and political intrigue. The memoirs of Horace Walpole, he observed, showed "how little those who live in public business, and of course in constant agitation and intrigue, know about the real and deep course of opinions and events." Such men as Walpole, on the fringes of power, "immersed in little political detail, and the struggling skirmish of party, seem to have lost sight of the great progressive movements of human affairs"—just as a miller might become so absorbed in his work that he failed to notice the gradual rising of the stream until it swept his mill away.[23]

As that remark suggests, the Waverley Novels imply a belief in "progress," if not an enthusiastic commitment. "Progress," for Scott, seems to consist in the transition of society from a barbarous to a civilized state, from superstition to reason, from tradition to fact, from violence to law, from personal to contractual relationships. The Highlands (before the uprising of 1745) stood for barbarism, the Great Britain of his own day for civilization. In the English compromise of ordered liberty, progress had apparently reached its conclusion, and further change could only be destructive. Energy and "enthusiasm" —fanatical commitment to a belief or a cause—are to be feared. Scott and his readers had seen their destructive effects in a generation of constant war and upheaval, in which the foundations of society had seemed to be in danger from the "enthusiasm" of revolutionary ideologues, a time when (at least to patriotic Britons) England had often seemed to stand alone against chaos. Napoleon himself might almost seem a "dark hero," and just as Scott and his readers were fascinated by the energy of his dark heroes, so Englishmen (including Sir Walter Scott, who spent years in writing his three-volume biography of the emperor) were fascinated in spite of themselves by the Napoleonic legend.

These "great progressive movements" of history are constantly in motion, even during periods of outward calm. "Great men" do not control them. Scott presents the "great" often enough, but never shows them in the act of consciously directing and guiding historical events. They are the agents of history, not its makers. In the earlier novels especially, Scott is extremely tactful in his presentation of great men. Writing such a book as Marguerite Yourcenar's *Memoirs of Hadrian*, a supposed autobiography of a Roman emperor, would have seemed highly presumptuous to him. In his treatment of the "great," Scott's approach seems close to Tolstoy's, in *War and Peace*, although he would not have accepted Tolstoy's doctrine that history is unintelligible, or his complete denial of the role of individuals in shaping it.

The basic theme of Scott's most characteristic work is itself historical: the conflict of the past and the present (the "present" of each particular novel, that is). Scott himself implied as much when he explained in his introduction to *The Fortunes of Nigel* that "the most picturesque period of history is that when the ancient rough and wild manners of a barbarous age are just becoming innovated upon and contrasted by the illumination of increased or revived learning and the instructions of renewed or reformed religion." Such periods offered the widest possible range of character and incident.

Such a contrast appears in every one of the "Scotch Novels" and in many of the later works. Of all Scott critics, Coleridge has best explained its significance:

Scott's great merit . . . lies in the nature of the subject . . . the contest between the loyalists and their opponents [Coleridge is apparently thinking of Jacobites and Whigs] can never become obsolete, for it is the contest between religious adherence to the past and the ancient, the desire and admiration of permanence, on the one hand; and the passion for increase of knowledge, for truth, as the offspring of reason—in short, the mighty instincts of *progression* and *free agency*, on the other. In all subjects of deep and lasting interest, you will detect a struggle between two opposites, two polar forces, both of which are alike necessary to our human well-being, and necessary each to the continued existence of the other.[24]

This conflict, adds Coleridge, creates "that equilibrium in which our moral Being subsists; while the disturbance of the same constitutes our sense of life." The "dark hero" is always associated with an older, more reckless, violent, and also more glamorous mode of life, and he must perish with it. The conflict is rich and suggestive, and its significance should not be limited to political attitudes. As Leslie Fiedler has shown, it can be expressed in Freudian terms: the contrasting heroes may represent "the principles of obedience and subversion, the controlled of the super-ego and the impulsive life of the id."[25] John Buchan has credited Scott with reviving memory of the two strands of Scottish history—the aristocratic and Cavalier; the Covenanting and democratic—and with preventing a newly prosperous and expanding Scotland from forgetting its past. But if this were the primary concern of the novels, they would have had little interest outside of Scotland. The broader theme suggested by Coleridge, the conflict between tradition, or reaction, and innovation, accounts more adequately both for the immediate success and for the enduring appeal of the Waverley Novels.

Here we can find a deeper explanation for Scott's long-continued interest in the Jacobite movement than merely his sympathy for a gallant and picturesque lost cause. Three novels—*Rob Roy*, *Waverley*, and *Redgauntlet*—carry the story of Jacobitism through the unsuccessful risings of 1715 and 1745 and on to the time in the 1760s when it was on the point of becoming merely an exercise in nostalgia, a harmless drinking of toasts to the "King over the water" or a chorus of "Charlie is my darling, the young chevalier." Jacobitism had attempted, coming surprisingly near success, to restore the past and to reestablish Scotland as a separate kingdom. Intellectually, Scott believed that events had worked out for the best. He valued the new security and prosperity of Scotland and saw that his own time was more comfortable, more rational, and more humane than the past. Rationally he was a Hanoverian, a Whig. Emotionally he was a Jacobite, attracted by the glamour of the Stuarts (a quality strikingly absent in the first three Georges), regretting the lost independence of Scotland, a loss that seemed to endanger all of its national characteristics and institutions. For similar reasons, Scott disliked reformers like Francis Jeffrey, who seemed to him to be trying to destroy everything that had made Scotland Scottish. The tension created in the works themselves is rooted in this division of sympathy, this split between head and heart, reason and emotion, in the author.

Politics

Scott's sense of history was inseparably related to his lifelong Toryism. His political thought is close to that of Edmund Burke; like Burke, he is prepared to accept and defend the results of past revolutions, but he deplores further change. Out of the conflicting fanaticisms of the past had emerged, in characteristically British fashion, a sensible middle way—one often represented by Scott's heroes and institutionalized by the Glorious Revolution of 1688, which had achieved a final settlement of the political order. His essential conservatism is aptly illustrated by his attitude toward the French Revolution. Unlike many of the other major writers of his time—Wordsworth, Coleridge, Blake, Byron, Shelley—Scott never expressed sympathy for the revolution or its aims. "Bliss was it in that dawn to be alive," Wordsworth might write, but the young Scott, far from feeling bliss, was drilling with the Edinburgh Volunteers to repel a French invasion and to intimidate the lower classes.

Never an "intellectual" in the usual sense of the word, Scott was skeptical of the Whiggish and liberal reliance on the power of abstract reason to achieve political progress. In 1810 he published a highly Burkean "Essay on Judicial Reform" in which he warned against the danger of a purely rationalistic analysis of existing institutions or laws: "the people have, by degrees, moulded their habits to the law they are compelled to obey,"[26] and innovations raised great danger of new and unforeseeable evils.

The kind of insight that his philosophy of history allowed and the limitations that it imposed are both revealed by his remark in his journal entry for 25 November 1825 (apropos of the growing agitation for Catholic Emancipation and parliamentary reform): "The Whigs will live and die in the heresy that the world is ruled by little pamphlets and speeches,"[27] and in their confidence that men only need to have their true interests explained to them in order to act accordingly. In reality, each man acts in accordance with his impulses, regardless of his own or the general welfare. But if liberals have often proved disastrously in error as a result of failing to allow for the power of the irrational in politics (as the history of the twentieth century demonstrates beyond any doubt), Scott was seriously mistaken in denying the effect of ideas on history. Such a denial barred him from understanding the "great progressive movements" of his own time, and prevented him from recognizing the significance of the supreme historical event of his age, the French Revolution.

Essential to Scott's Toryism was an intense respect for order and degree, as necessary to a stable society. (In this respect at least, he seems close to the Shakespeare of the history plays.) Scott held a profound respect for the duke of Buccleuch, traditional head of the Scott clan, and at Abbotsford he seems to have intended to create an almost feudal estate, in which his tenants and workmen would owe him unquestioning loyalty and obedience, while he would be morally obliged to guard their physical and spiritual welfare and shield them from dangerous ideas. The gloom of Scott's last years was due not only to his bankruptcy and his failing health but also to the course of public events—to his dismay at the "insatiable appetite of innovation" that seemed to characterize the age.

Agitation for the Reform Bill, extending the right to vote and eliminating "rotten boroughs" (parliamentary districts that had lost most of their population), and giving representation to the new towns of the industrial age seemed to him to threaten social and political chaos. Against such a danger, almost any measures seemed justified. Learning that troops had fired over the heads of demonstrators instead of directly at them, Scott complained that "in such cases severity is ultimate mercy." As the public crisis intensified, with a new revolution in France, he elaborated in his journal a political fantasy more improbable than anything in his novels. With the rightful king deposed and replaced by a relative with liberal tendency, as had happened in France— "Then what would be the remedy? Marry! Seize on the Person of the Princess Vittoria [the future Queen Victoria], carrying her North and setting up the banner of England with the Duke of W [Wellington] as Dictator."[28] Chaos seemed come again.

Scott is equally conservative in his moral and religious thought. The moral code of the Waverley Novels is strict, based on restraint and self-denial— Victorian before Victoria. Anthony Trollope praised Scott for the "strain" he put upon himself so that "he should not be carried away into the seducing language of ill-regulated passion,"[29] and certainly such language is not to be found in the novels. It is doubtful, though, that excluding it imposed any "strain" on the author. Scott's heroes are never seriously tempted by "ill-regulated passion," and his biographers provide no evidence that he himself was ever so tempted.

Scott's religious beliefs, as implied in the novels, appear superficial and conventional. Catholicism both attracts and repels; its picturesque ceremonies appealed to the imagination and to the emotions, but the old Scottish prejudices against popery are strong—in *Ivanhoe*, for example. Scott himself was satisfied with a comfortable and undemanding Episcopalianism. A passage in *Waverley* seems unconsciously revealing: "This worthy man . . . preached the practical fruits of Christianity as well as its abstract tenets." That sentence roused Coleridge to indignation: "*Abstract tenets*—i.e., whatever in the Gospel is peculiar to the Gospel! O what an opening into the actual state of religion among the higher classes. . . . Christ's Divinity, the Fall of Man, Sin, Redemption—abstract tenets!"[30]

Those doctrines would not have been "abstract tenets" to the Cameronians of *Old Mortality*; such an easy dismissal barred Scott from sympathy with and full understanding of many of the scenes and characters from Scottish history that he chose to present. But the conservative Scott could never be quite at ease with either the fervent piety or the implicit democracy of Scottish Presbyterianism. He had no interest in theology, and his own piety was unemotional; he seems to have valued religion chiefly as a necessary protection for morality and the social order. His own deepest belief, often expressed in his journal during his last years, was an entirely non-Christian fatalism, a stoical acceptance of whatever might come.

Hazlitt's comment, in *The Spirit of the Age*, that "The old world is to him a crowded map; the new one a dull, hateful blank. He dotes on all well-authenticated superstitions; he shudders at the shadow of innovation," is a melodramatic exaggeration. Scott certainly feared innovation, yet he furnished Abbotsford with the latest modern conveniences and he presided over an Oil Gas Company that proposed to light Edinburgh with gas. Neither did he dote on every aspect of the past. Still, the Waverley Novels could easily be read as Hazlitt read them, and Hazlitt is probably right in claiming that this interpretation aided Scott's popularity: "The political bearing of the Scotch Novels has been a considerable recommendation to them. They are a relief to the mind, rarified as it has been with modern philosophy, and heated with ultra-radicalism." That suggestion is amusingly supported by Stendhal's novel, *La Chartreuse de Parme* (*The Charter-House of Parma*) whose young hero, a worshipper of Napoleon, is forbidden, during the intellectual reaction that followed Napoleon's defeat, to read any book written later than 1715—except the Waverley Novels!

The Ideology of Status

In the Waverley Novels an ordered society is the highest political and social value, and for Scott this meant a society in which the social hierarchy is carefully preserved—although by law and custom rather than by force. The Scott hero often seems hardly an individual at all, he is Everygentleman, the representative of an ideology of status. Consequently the heroes are almost all alike. As a British gentleman of the early nineteenth century, whatever his ostensible period (the heroes and heroines are the least historically accurate figures in the Waverley Novels), he must display extreme respect for property, law, and the constituted authorities. Those who try to deny him his status or to deprive him of it are enemies of society, villains by definition.

Character, manners, even ancient lineage, do not make the gentleman. Property is required—landed property, with the solidity and stability it implies. Money alone will not do. Above all, the hero must not *earn* his wealth. (In *Rob Roy*, Frank Osbaldistone might become rich simply from his father's business, but he must become a landed proprietor as well, even if his uncle and seven cousins need to be disposed of before he can inherit the family estate.) The only profession allowable is war; Lovel and Brown-Bertram are both soldiers when they first appear, and Brown-Bertram proves his innate gentlemanliness when (knowing nothing of his family and his heritage, and brought up as a Dutchman) he gives up commerce at the first opportunity to enlist in the British army. Scott's standard is unusually strict for his time—Jane Austen's heroes could also be sailors or clergymen of the Church of England. The businessman, again by definition, cannot be a gentleman; Scott was aware also of how earned wealth might subvert the social order. (He used his own earned wealth to buy an estate and assimilate himself to the aristocracy.)

In this conservatism lies an explanation of the curious passivity of the Scott hero, whose respect for the rights of property and the power of the established authority is so exaggerated that it paralyzes him. This is why the Scott hero can never be a convincing rebel, even when circumstances require it. Waverley and Henry Morton do join rebellions, but only through overwhelming force of circumstances. Their main concern appears to be to protect friends on the other side, and they are thoroughly uncomfortable until other circumstances disengage them. (The radical Cameronians of *Old Mortality* were quite right to distrust Morton. He was never one of them.)

Gentlemanliness is a negative quality—the gentleman is distinguished by the number of things that he does not do. He does not earn money, of course; neither does he examine his feelings, or display them. Unlike the dark heroes, he does not become passionate, either in love or in anger. Being a gentleman, he must preserve or be restored to his rightful property in order to hold or acquire his proper status, and property depends on law and on unquestioning submission to it—that is, on passivity. Violence necessarily threatens order, and in Scott's novels, those who practice it, in whatever cause, must die—at least, if they are gentlemen. The hero, then, can be a soldier; he can fight a duel and wound his opponent, but he does not kill.

In *Old Mortality* the villainous Basil Oliphant must be killed—but the task has to be performed by the hero's servant, Cuddie Headrigg. (Oliphant has never appeared in the novel up to this scene, but he is a villain by definition, and deserving death, because he is trying to dispossess the Bellenden family of their rightful estate.) Villains threaten the established order, and so do the dark heroes, with their dangerous energies. The passivity of the hero is absolute; it threatens nothing. And perhaps it performs a positive function as well. One recent critic suggests that the opening chapters of *Old Mortality*, for example, "present a carefully organized series of tests," narrowing the field of possibilities until Morton has no alternative left but to join the rebels. "It is the role of the Waverley hero . . . to hold off this remorseless narrowing, to keep the bridge open between choices."[31]

Critics have frequently complained of a lack of depth in Scott's characters, and at least one admirer has tried, rather absurdly, to make a virtue out of this deficiency: "He had a fine reticence that forbade his disclosing either his own innermost personal feelings or those of his characters." The suggestion by one of his biographers, H. J. C. Grierson, seems more plausible: "If he did not enter very deeply into the souls of the characters whom he drew, it was because he never entered very deeply into his own motives. . . . It is this dislike of analyzing feeling that makes his heroes of so little interest."[32] The personal explanation may well be true, but it might be added that if the hero is to play the ideological role of every gentleman, he cannot be strongly individualized, he can hardly have a complex inner life.

Scott was surely one of the least introspective of major novelists, so ignorant of his own nature that after ten years of extravagant spending and constantly accumulating debt, he could solemnly warn his eldest son: "You must learn to keep all your expenses within your income; it is a lesson which, if not learned in youth, lays up much bitter regret for age."[33] The reader of the Waverley Novels will learn a good deal about Scott's interests, but little about his personality or the details of his life: Scott never wrote a *David Copperfield* or a *Pendennis.* That lack of interest in himself is paralleled by a lack of concern with aesthetic issues. His letters make dull reading, they reveal nothing of either his inner life or of his literary concerns. (The journal, mostly written after the disaster of bankruptcy, is far more revealing and therefore more interesting.)

Carlyle's comment on the Waverley Novels, that "The great fact about them is that they were faster written and better paid for than any other books in the world,"[34] merely states what Scott would have considered the evidence of his success. In writing of Dryden's plays, he described his own qualities as a novelist: "Laborious accuracy of expression, and fine traits of character, joined to an action which should be at once pleasing, interesting, and probable, required sedulous study, deep reflection, and long and repeated correction and revision. But these were not to be expected from a playwright, by whom three dramas were to be produced in one season; and in their place were substituted adventures, surprises, rencounters [*sic*], mistakes, disguises, and escapes."[35] Change "playwright" to "novelist" and "dramas" to "novels," and the passage applies exactly to Scott.

Many readers are bored and irritated by concern with form, or with moral issues, or by analysis—even passion can disturb them. Adventures, surprises, and escapes are exactly what they require. Coleridge assumed that the weaknesses of the Waverley Novels were essential to their mass popularity, pointing out that Scott's fiction made fewer demands on the reader than the great novels of Fielding and Richardson: "The absence of the higher beauties . . . of style, character, and plot has done more for Sir Walter Scott's European . . . popularity, than ever the abundance of them effected for any former writer."[36] In an "age of anxiety" (Coleridge's own phrase), like the early nineteenth century, readers sought escape on the easiest terms.

The Waverley Novels of course also possessed qualities lacking in other contemporary fiction—the Gothic novel or the novel of manners, as practiced by Jane Austen and other female writers—and also in the eighteenth-century classics. And while Scott did not originate the intellectual reaction against rationalism and Jacobinism and the increasing concern for tradition and the past, the growing sense of nationalism and interest in the history of one's own nation or region, his work both strengthened and appealed to those tendencies.

Other reasons for the success of the novels are easy to suggest. The mystery of at least theoretically anonymous authorship added to public curiosity and encouraged discussion. As Carlyle observed, "The Waverley Novels circulated and reigned triumphant; to the general imagination the 'Author of Waverley' was like some living mythological personage and ranked among the chief wonders of the world." (No wonder Scott valued even a partial anonymity: "Sir Walter Scott, Baronet," could never compete with that imposing figure.) The novels met the requirements of their time. In his respect for propriety, for example, Scott was far superior to his eighteenth-century predecessors—a matter of great importance in an age of tightening moral standards, with Victorianism only a few years away and reading aloud in the family circle a favorite amusement. The works were proper, the author was a gentleman, and that, as Adolphus pointed out, was distressingly rare among authors: "How few there are who give any proof in their works of the refined taste, the instinctive sense of propriety, the clear spirit of honour . . . the familiar acquaintance with conventional forms of good breeding, which are essential to the character of a gentleman!"[37]

Best of all, the novels offered an ideal escape to the comfortable and respectable reader. A character like Rob Roy, Leslie Fiedler has pointed out, "projects the bourgeois' own slight margin of resentment against the safe, commercial way of life he has desired, and for which, indeed, he would fight. . . . Such tame outsiders represent the impulsive and the irrational only as a passing temptation . . . not as a profound threat."[38] A Waverley or a Frank Osbaldistone may tour the wild Highlands and feel the dangerous glamour of a dark hero, but he soon returns, with souvenirs and regrets, to England or to the Lowlands, to common sense and respectability.

Reputation

Criticism of the Waverley Novels began with the publication of *Waverley* in 1814, and continued in an abundant stream through the nineteenth century, then in steadily diminishing volume for several decades, increasing again, at an accelerating rate, since the mid-1960s. His contemporaries, with only a few exceptions like Coleridge, had no doubt that he was the greatest of novelists. To express their sense of his greatness, his English admirers paid his work the highest compliment they could imagine—they compared it with Shakespeare's, a comparison that became standard for many years and has been made in the twentieth century by such admirers as Grierson and David Daiches. Scott wrote historical novels and Shakespeare had written historical plays; both were prolific and rapid writers, and presumably careless about revision (according to Ben Jonson's report, Shakespeare was reputed to have "never blotted a line"); Shakespeare was a successful man of the theater as Scott was a successful man of letters.

More often than not, the comparison turns out to be a critical strategy for reducing the importance of what were commonly considered to be Scott's weaknesses, or even for elevating them into virtues, by attributing them to Shakespeare. In any case, the differences of period and of medium are so great that the comparison is generally unilluminating. *Old Mortality*, writes one admirer of the Waverley Novels, is "the kind of story which was his, and Shakespeare's, normal method of presenting life and history—a broadly delineated chapter of history with strongly marked characters, natural and intelligible, but not too deeply or subtly analyzed."[39] That statement may be true of the author of *Waverley*, but is it true of the author of *Hamlet*?

Comparisons with Cervantes' *Don Quixote* seem more appropriate. Scott was familiar with *Don Quixote*, and there is a similar theme in much of his work: "Novel after novel presents an illusioned, romantic young man pursuing a series of exotic adventures in a dreamlike trance. . . . Eventually . . . he comes out of his dream with a sensation of sadness and loss."[40] Waverley is no doubt the purest example of such an "illusioned" young man. Occasionally there is the wily, practical, sometimes rascally servant, like Andrew Fairservice in *Rob Roy* or Cuddie Headrigg in *Old Mortality* who accompany their unworldly young masters as Sancho Panza accompanies Quixote. Free from gentlemanly scruples, they have the useful ability to lie when necessary and even (like Cuddie) to kill.

Well before Scott's death, a critical consensus about his work had been reached: "His characters are superior to his plots; his humble, to his higher life; his Scotland to his England; his tragedy to his comedy; and, in general, his earlier to his later works." Carelessness in plotting and solecisms in his language were widely admitted, but considered unimportant. Reinforced by the admiration for Scott's character that developed during his last years and was strongly reinforced by Lockhart's biography, this attitude prevailed well past the middle of the nineteenth century.

Carlyle's vicious attack, published as a review of Lockhart's biography, was the most striking exception, charging Scott with commercialism, with superficiality of characterization, with writing by formula (he "manufactures," rather than "creates," claimed Carlyle), and above all with lack of seriousness. The Waverley Novels offered no message to their readers, their author "wished not the world to elevate itself, to amend itself, to do this or to do that, except simply pay him for books he kept writing." For Robert Louis Stevenson (whose *Kidnapped* and *The Master of Ballantrae* could hardly have been written without the example of the Waverley Novels) Scott failed in aesthetic seriousness, rather than moral earnestness, as Carlyle would have it. Scott, for Stevenson, was a "great daydreamer" rather than an artist—hardly an artist at all: "he conjured up the romantic with delight but had hardly the patience to describe it."[41]

Henry James, the historian of "fine consciousness," endlessly analytical, might seem at the opposite extreme from Scott, yet his comments are both more generous and more understanding than Stevenson's. For James, Scott is an archetypal novelist, like Balzac and Dickens, one of the great practitioners, the "fine painters of life."[42] And his criticism is surprisingly mild: if Scott's novels lacked "architecture," or Jamesian form, they at least were built of the best materials. James could hardly be satisfied with the Scott hero, of course. Edgar Ravenswood, he observes, may be a Hamlet in his black cloak and hat and plume, but he is a Hamlet without a mind, and consequently there is a sacrifice of intensity in the presentation of his love for Lucy Ashton—"the centre of the subject is empty," although, James adds, the "frame" is "beautifully rich and curious."[43] But this, he suggests elsewhere, may be a deficiency of the English novel; not only Scott but Jane Austen, Dickens, and Thackeray had all represented young people in love with each other, but always a love without passion.

Writers of the early twentieth century, revolting against the nineteenth-century tradition, could not afford such tolerance. E. M. Forster mounted a sustained attack in his *Aspects of the Novel*. Scott displayed "a trivial mind and a heavy style. He cannot construct. He has neither artistic detachment nor passion, and how can a writer who is devoid of both, create characters who will move us deeply? . . . think how all Scott's laborious mountains and scooped-out glens call out for passion, passion and how it is never there! . . . he only has temperate and gentlemanly feelings and an intelligent affection for the country-side; and this is not basis enough for great novels." Forster's conclusion, that "to make one thing happen after another is his only serious aim,"[44] is surely not an adequate account of the novels, although it might well have been accepted by the author. The absence of passion applies primarily to the official hero and heroine (compare any Waverley Novel with *Wuthering Heights* or *Jane Eyre* or *The Return of the Native*).

F. R. Leavis, a creator of the modernist canon and a dominant critic of the thirties and forties, could hardly be expected to admire Scott. Yet his judgment, although basically similar to Forster's, is surprisingly mild, from a critic noted for severity. Leavis finds Scott "an inspired folklorist"—not very different from Forster's phrase, "an intelligent affection for the country-side"—and finds that "the heroics of the historical novel can no longer command respect. He was a great and very intelligent man; but, not having the creative writer's interest in literature, he made no serious attempt to work out his own form. . . . *The Heart of Midlothian* comes the nearest to being a great novel, but hardly is that: too many allowances and deductions have to be made."[45] The only parts of Scott's work that retain any vitality for Leavis are "The Two Drovers" and "Wandering Willie's Tale."

But for the greater part of the twentieth century, Scott has been ignored rather than condemned by critics. Not surprisingly, the greatest enthusiasm for his work has been shown by his own countrymen, who have a natural interest in his subject matter and a patriotic enthusiasm for his reputation as one of the two great writers of modern Scotland—a prose counterpart of Burns. Scott himself provided an explanation of this kind of popularity in commenting on the appeal of "our popular poetry." Readers are "charmed by the effect of local description, and sometimes impute that effect to the poet, which is produced by the recollections and associations which his verses excite." And certainly readers familiar with spoken Scots seem best qualified to appreciate the Scotch novels.

It may seem paradoxical that some of the most sympathetic and influential modern criticism of Scott's work should have been written by George Lukács, probably the best-known Marxist critic of the twentieth century, but Scott, like Marx, views society as a product of history. For Lukács, Scott is a great popular writer, in spite of his conservative ideology. His presentation of characters drawn from the lower classes is unprecedented, both in their importance and in the sympathy and detail with which they are presented. And he is the first novelist to be intelligently concerned with history—to Scott, a historical crisis is a kind of dialectical conflict between opposing forces, resulting in a new synthesis. Thus the conflict between Norman and Saxon produces the Englishman, represented by Wilfrid of Ivanhoe. Scott among novelists first saw the necessary involvement of individual life with historical process; "historicity itself, the fated personal entanglement with historic forces," becomes for him the subject of the Waverley Novels.

The critical neglect, or comparative neglect of Scott's novels ended in the mid-1960s, and an outpouring of academic criticism (stimulated in part by significant anniversaries, the two hundredth of Scott's birth and the one hundred fiftieth of his death) has continued ever since, in monographs, articles, and critical symposia, while general works on the English novel have begun to examine the influence of Scott with unaccustomed attention. (George Levine's *The Realistic Imagination: English Fiction from Frankenstein to Lady Chatterley*, for example, sees the Waverley Novels as providing "the primary insights upon which realism in the nineteenth century developed, accompanied by a powerful distrust of fictions.")[46] Alexander Welsh's *The Hero of the Waverley Novels* (1963) inaugurated the trend (although Welsh is clearly indebted to Leslie Fiedler's discussion of blonde and brunette stereotyping in his *Love and Death in the American Novel*), and Welsh's analysis of the passive hero as embodying and expressing an ideology of status, a concept of the gentleman and his place in an ordered society, has influenced nearly all later criticism. In the seventies and eighties, female scholars have increasingly turned their attention to Scott. Jane Millgate presents a detailed and highly sympathetic study of the "Scotch Novels" in *Walter Scott: The Making of the Novelist* (1984), focusing on the novelistic innovations introduced by Scott, while Judith Wilt's innovative *Secret Leaves: The Novels of Walter Scott* (1985) proposes that the Waverley Novels dramatize "the victory of two linked 'modern' principles, male rationality and textualized language, over their progenitors, female enchantment or mystery and performative speech."[47]

Influence

Certainly no student of literature and the novel (and not only the English novel) can afford to ignore the Waverley Novels. Scott's influence on world literature may well have been greater than that of any other British writer of the past two centuries, with Byron and Dickens as the only possible competitors. Walter Allen, in his history of the English novel (1954), sums up the effects of Scott's work: "He made the European novel"; "he revolutionized the writing of history"; "in religion . . . he lay behind the Oxford movement."[48] That order may seem anticlimactic, but undoubtedly Scott's work significantly affected the minds of men like Newman and Ruskin, and encouraged the fashionable medievalism of the Victorian Age. And in politics, Scott perhaps did as much as Edmund Burke to create a philosophic Toryism, viewing society and the state as organisms developing through time—not merely as made up of a body of laws that could easily be rewritten and rationalized.

Scott's influence on the writing of history was profound. History was still a literary as well as a scholarly genre, and certainly the great narrative historians of nineteenth-century England and America—Macaulay, Carlyle, Prescott, Parkman—who aimed at making history as concrete, picturesque, and exciting as fiction, owed a large debt to the Waverley Novels both for their methods and for the audience that bought their books. Scott's novels broadened the concept of history to include social and cultural development as well as politics and war. When Scott had delighted readers with his lower-class characters and his broad canvasses of past societies and cultures, historians could follow suit, concerning themselves not only with recording names and dates, but with re-creating vanished cultures. And so Macaulay began his *History of England*, which sold almost as well as the Waverley Novels had done, with an elaborate and unprecedented survey of late seventeenth-century English society at all levels before proceeding to his political narrative.

But Scott's literary influence is more important still. "He made the European novel"—to a surprising extent, that claim is literally true. The first important modern Italian novel, Alessandro Manzoni's *The Betrothed* (1825), set in Milan of the early seventeenth century and centering on a pair of peasant lovers, is directly inspired by the Waverley Novels. Manzoni admitted, in fact, that he would never have thought of writing a novel if he had not read Scott. And in the mid-twentieth century, Giuseppe di Lampedusa's *The Leopard Prince*, a novel set in 1859–60, the period of the unification of Italy, offers "the passive hero round whom the action circulates," though Lampedusa's Leopard prince is far superior in intelligence and sensitivity to Scott's heroes. But in Lampedusa's novel as in *Waverley*, a political and social order is about to be destroyed. As one critic observes, in *The Leopard Prince* "We see how the Garibaldian invasion of Sicily expressed a historical spirit against which the feudal monarchy proved as feeble a bulwark as the Highland clan system was against the encroachments of the commercial spirit of the eighteenth century."[49]

The case is the same in Russia, where Scott's influence led directly to the first significant Russian novel, Alexander Pushkin's *The Captain's Daughter*

(1836), which deals with a peasant uprising in the late eighteenth century—
just the sort of subject typical of Scott. Pushkin's rather colorless hero suggests the Waverley hero, and Pugachov, the violent and brutal leader of the
rebellion, has a good deal in common with Scott's dark heroes. One might
think also of Nikolai Gogol's novel of seventeenth-century Cossack life,
Taras Bulba (1835), and above all of Tolstoy's *War and Peace* (1869). Scott
had shown the way to present both a public and a private story in the same
work (as he had done notably in *Old Mortality*, with the public story of the
Cameronians' rebellion, and the private history of Morton), to mingle historical and fictional characters, giving equal vitality to both, and to demonstrate
the influence of history, the public story, on the imagined characters of the
private story.

The Waverley Novels exerted an even stronger influence on the sup-
pressed nationalities of Eastern Europe. Modern Hungarian literature begins
in the 1830s with imitations of Scott, and in Poland, somewhat later, there
are the novels of Henryk Sienkiwiecz, written at a time when the Polish nation had not existed for a century, that presented Poland's successful struggle
for survival during the seventeenth century against apparently overwhelming
odds. Written for people who had nearly forgotten their history, such novels
functioned as culture-creating, nation-building works.

The influence of the Waverley Novels spread even farther; the British carried Scott to India, and the first Bengali novel, Bankim Chatterjee's *The
Chieftain's Daughter* (1865), a historical novel set in the sixteenth century,
derives its plot and characters from *Ivanhoe*. Like Ivanhoe, the Hindu hero is
loved by two women, one of them of his own religion. But when he is
wounded and held captive by the Moslem enemy, the passionate Ayesha, a
Moslem, cares for the prisoner and falls in love with him in spite of the im-
passable religious barrier. Chatterjee went on to become a fervent nationalist.
To a member of a conquered people, Scott's novel carried revolutionary
implications.

French literature, of course, was far more highly developed, yet Scott's influence is strong and unmistakable. The enthusiasm of the public for the
Waverley Novels was satirized by a contemporary: "By Walter Scott! By
Walter Scott! Hurry, gentlemen and especially ladies; it's marvelous, it's new;
hurry! The first edition is exhausted, the second is sold in advance, the third
will disappear as soon as it leaves the press. Run, buy; good or bad, what does
it matter! Sir Walter Scott has put his name to it, and that's enough."[50]
Scott's influence is clear in the historical fiction of Dumas, Alfred de Vigny,
Prosper Merimee, and Theophile Gautier, among others. Balzac's first important novel, *Les Chouans* (1829), dealt with civil war between revolution-

aries and monarchists during the French Revolution—just the sort of subject that fascinated Scott—as does Victor Hugo's *Quatre-vingt-treize* (Ninety-three). And Hugo's massive re-creation of medieval France in *Notre Dame de Paris* (*The Hunchback of Notre Dame*, in English translations) in 1831 could hardly have been written without the example of *Ivanhoe* and *Quentin Durward*.

As for Balzac, his enormous *Comedie humaine*, a panorama of French life in the second quarter of the nineteenth century and one of the monuments of nineteenth-century European literature, would hardly have been possible without Scott's presentation of society as essentially organic, and of social and ideological forces as continuously shaping not only the lives but the consciousness of all its members. Reading Scott showed Balzac the need for "revealing man in his public and social aspects, man as shaped by his place and function in society, and his relation to a historic past."[51] (That lesson was basic to Victorian realism as well.) Even a writer as consciously hostile to Scott's work as Stendhal seems to have been affected. His *Chartreuse de Parme* (1840), although nearly contemporary in its setting, is certainly an attempt to re-create a vanished society, and the famous description of the hero, Fabrizio, at Waterloo (Fabrizio reaches the field just as the French army is breaking up, never glimpses his idol, Napoleon, never fires a shot, and finally asks himself if he has really been in a battle) may have been suggested by Scott's frequently oblique approach to a great historic event or figure.

Scott's influence was not confined to the novel. Painters chose subjects from the Waverley Novels, and so did composers. Scott himself saw an opera based on *Ivanhoe*, with music drawn from Rossini operas, during his Paris visit of 1826. There were ten operatic versions of *Ivanhoe*, nine each of *The Bride of Lammermoor* and of *Kenilworth* (both novels offered that favorite operatic theme, a tragic love story), and four of *The Talisman*, among many others. Of them all, Donizetti's *Lucia di Lammermoor* (1835) remains a favorite, and Bellini's *I Puritani* (distantly based on *Old Mortality*) is still performed. Often they were given with elaborate staging and scenery, for which Scott's novels invariably provided occasion.

Certainly no grand opera could ever have been grander than Sir Arthur Sullivan's *Ivanhoe* (this is the Sullivan of Gilbert and Sullivan, who longed to write a serious opera), performed in 1891 with an enormous orchestra and cast, in a theater especially intended to house the British National Opera, for an unprecedented run of 160 nights. That production was a political rather than a musical event (Sullivan's *Ivanhoe* promptly disappeared from the operatic repertoire), expressing the patriotic imperialism of late nineteenth-century England and stressing English unity at a time when the lower orders of society seemed restless and the socialist threat caused much anxiety. Scott's influence was not limited to Europe. The American novel really begins with the work of Fenimore Cooper—"the American Scott," he was called. Cooper owes nearly everything—style, subject, character types—to Scott. After beginning with an imitation of Jane Austen, in his second and third novels, *The Spy* (1821) and *Lionel Lincoln* (1825), Cooper turned to the national past for his subject. He chose the heroic period of American history, the Revolution—which was also a period of divided loyalties, and as in Scott, each novel contains a protagonist who is able to maintain relations with both sides. In his most important work, the five Leatherstocking Tales, Cooper finds his greatest subject, a representative American subject more imaginatively significant than the Revolution. That subject is the frontier, Cooper's equivalent for the Highland Line, dividing civilization from barbarism, the present from the past. (As in Scott, the past is doomed, a fate that is intellectually accepted but emotionally resisted.) This line his characters must cross, in his most popular and influential novels, before the true action can commence. It is possible to see in Scott's Edie Ochiltree a prototype of Cooper's Natty Bumppo, or "Leatherstocking," as he appears in *The Pioneers*, the first novels of the Leatherstocking series—both are old men who have spent all their lives as free wanderers, almost as parts of the natural world.

Less obvious, yet equally real, is the debt of Nathaniel Hawthorne, who delighted in the Waverley Novels throughout his life. Hawthorne's early and abortive project, "Seven Tales of My Native Land," was an attempt to do for New England's past what Scott had done for Scotland's, and in *The Scarlet Letter*, as well as in several of his finest tales, he accomplished his purpose. Similarities between Scott's Presbyterians and Hawthorne's Puritans seem obvious, but a deeper parallelism can be seen in Hawthorne's use, notably in *The Scarlet Letter* and "Young Goodman Brown," of the town-forest contrast, with the town as the area of "civilization," of law, morality, and conscience (even of consciousness), while the forest, where the Black Man of Puritan mythology walked, is the domain of Nature, of passion, fantasy, and dream.

A third major American writer, Mark Twain, also responded strongly to the influence of Scott—in his case, with ridicule, parody, and denunciation. Apparently basing his conception of "Scott" on a single work, *Ivanhoe*, Twain denounced his influence on the culture of the American South, infecting it with a false ideal of "chivalry"—which in practice meant uncontrolled violence. And Scott's prose style, with its polysyllabic pomposity and windy circumlocutions, had corrupted Southern writing and prevented the South from developing a truly modern literature. It is by no accident that the wrecked steamboat in *Huckleberry Finn*, on which Huck and Jim nearly lose their lives when they rashly go on board looking for adventure, should be named the *Walter Scott*. (There may or may not actually have been a *Walter Scott* on the Mississippi, but the owner of one line named every one of his boats after a Scott heroine.)

In *Life on the Mississippi*, Twain makes his major attack, blaming the influence of Scott for the American Civil War through the perversion of Southern character produced by his novels. His merciless burlesque of knighthood and the ideal of "chivalry" in *A Connecticut Yankee in King Arthur's Court*— notably in the tournament at Camelot in which the Yankee, armed with lasso and revolver, first defeats Sir Sagramor (knight and horse are described as "The iron tower and the gorgeous bedquilt"), then all the knights of the roundtable—probably owes at least as much to his reading of *Ivanhoe* as to his encounter with Malory's *Morte d'Arthur*.

The history of the Victorian novel, in England, would have been unimaginably different if the Waverley Novels had not been written. The historical novels of course—Thackeray's *Henry Esmond*, Dickens's *Barnaby Rudge* and *Tale of Two Cities*, even George Eliot's *Romola*—were made possible by the precedent of the Waverley Novels. Scott made regional peculiarities of custom and dialect acceptable in serious fiction, whereas in the eighteenth-century novel, and in the old drama, such characteristics had invariably been presented as inherently clownish, uncouth, and absurd. If we associate Thomas Hardy with "Wessex" or George Eliot and later D. H. Lawrence with the English Midlands, it is in part because Scott had provided the necessary example with his treatment of Lowland types speaking their native dialect.

Closely related is a still more important point—Scott's treatment of characters from the lower classes. It could be said without much exaggeration that in earlier literature it had been nearly impossible to treat such characters realistically. They had either been clowns, like Shakespeare's commoners, or the idealized nymphs and swains of pastoral poetry. It is not easy to imagine the startling novelty of a Jeanie Deans or a Dandie Dinmont in the first quarter of the nineteenth century. Contemporary readers, aware of the novelty, responded variously. The conservative, like a *Blackwoods* reviewer, found far too much about "the concerns of a cowfeeder and his daughter" and regretted such a tendency to deal "not only with low, but with vulgar life," whereby the Muse had "soiled her petticoats, if not dimmed her beauty."[52]

Another reviewer, writing for the more liberal *Edinburgh Review*, noted the

paradox that in spite of his "propensities decidedly aristocratic," Scott succeeded best "in the representation of homely characters;—and not in the ludicrous or contemptuous representation of them—but by showing them at
once more natural and more interesting than they had ever been made before
. . . by showing them not as clowns to be laughed at . . . but as human creatures." The finer qualities ascribed to them, the reviewer concluded, "are so
blended and harmonized with the native rudeness of their life and occupa-
tions, that they are made interesting and even noble beings . . . and delight us
without trespassing at all on the province of pastoral or romance."[53] Something may be owing to his Scottish background—Burns's poetry had been
far more democratic and socially inclusive than any English poetry of the
eighteenth century. Whatever the cause, Scott had achieved, in much of his
dialogue (but not in the dialogue of his English-speaking characters, or in his
own narration) what Wordsworth had attempted in poetry—"a selection of
language really used by men."

Above all, then, Scott was a great innovator: he developed the historical
novel, he made possible the serious presentation of regional characteristics,
including dialect, and of characters below the social level of the aristocracy
and the upper middle class. Scott enormously widened the range of fiction—
certainly no other writer would deserve a longer chapter in any history of either the English or the world novel.

Notes and References

Chapter One

1. 12 December 1825, *The Journal of Sir Walter Scott*, ed. W. E. K. Anderson (London: Oxford University Press, 1972), 43.
2. Thomas Carlyle, review of Lockhart's *Life of Sir Walter Scott, Bart*, reprinted in *Scott: The Critical Heritage*, ed. John O. Hayden (New York: Barnes & Noble, 1970), 371.

Chapter Two

1. John Gibson Lockhart, *Memoirs of the Life of Sir Walter Scott* (New York: Houghton Mifflin, 1901), 1:419.
2. Quoted in *Scott's Complete Poetical Works*, ed. H. E. Scudder (New York: Houghton Mifflin, 1898), 39.
3. H. J. C. Grierson, *Sir Walter Scott, Bart* (London: Constable, 1938), 81.
4. Quoted in *Scott: The Critical Heritage*, 39.
5. *The Letters of William and Dorothy Wordsworth: The Middle Years*, ed. Ernest De Selincourt (Oxford: Oxford University Press, 1937), 1:240.
6. Quoted in Lockhart, *Memoirs*, 2:171.
7. *Scott's Complete Poetical Works*, 152.
8. *Collected Letters of Samuel Taylor Coleridge*, ed. E. L. Griggs (Oxford: Oxford University Press 1956–71), 3:291.
9. John L. Adolphus, *Letters to Richard Heber, Esq.* (London: Rodell & Martin, 1822), 132.
10. *Coleridge the Talker*, ed. R. W. Armour and R. F. Howes (Ithaca, N.Y.: Cornell University Press, 1941), 171.
11. Jane Millgate, *Walter Scott: The Making of the Novelist* (Toronto: University of Toronto Press, 1984), 27.

Chapter Three

1. *Lives of the Novelists* (London: Oxford University Press, 1906), 21.
2. Ibid., 308.
3. Lockhart, *Memoirs*, 3:16.
4. *Journal*, 12 February 1826, 86.
5. Lockhart, *Memoirs*, 4:456.
6. *Journal*, 12 February 1826, 86.
7. Lockhart, *Memoirs*, 3:22.
8. *Journal*, 18 December 1825, 40.

9. Quoted in Hesketh Pearson, *Sir Walter Scott: His Life and Personality* (London: Methuen, 1954), 242.

10. *Journal*, 12 April 1829, 554.

11. *Lives of the Novelists*, 18–19.

12. Review of *Emma*, *Quarterly Review* 14 (1814):199.

13. Ibid., 195.

14. Ibid., 197.

15. *Journal*, 14 March 1826, 114.

16. Ibid., 18 September 1827, 353.

17. Review of *Frankenstein*, *Blackwood's Magazine* 2 (1818):613.

18. Ibid.

19. *Lives of the Novelists*, 252.

20. George Levine, *The Realistic Imagination: English Fiction from Frankenstein to Lady Chatterley* (Chicago: University of Chicago Press, 1981), 17.

Chapter Four

1. General preface to the Waverley Novels.

2. Ibid.

3. Ibid.

4. John W. Croker, review of *Waverley*, *Quarterly Review*, July 1814, 377.

5. Francis Jeffrey, review of *Waverley*, *Edinburgh Review*, November 1814, reprinted in *Scott: The Critical Heritage*, 79.

6. Quoted in Lockhart, *Memoirs*, 2:534–35.

7. Jeffrey, review of *Waverley*, 79.

8. Quoted in *Scott: The Critical Heritage*, 75.

9. *Jane Austen's Letters to Her Sister Cassandra and Others*, ed. R. W. Chapman (London: Oxford University Press, 1952), 404.

10. Quoted in Lockhart, *Memoirs*, 2:171.

11. Ibid., 2:396.

12. Quoted in *Scott: The Critical Heritage*, 75.

13. Martin Meisel, "*Waverley*, Freud, and Topographical Metaphor," *University of Toronto Quarterly*, Spring 1979, 234.

14. Quoted in James T. Hillhouse, *The Waverley Novels and Their Critics* (Minneapolis: University of Minnesota Press, 1936), 112.

15. In *Sir Walter Scott Lectures*, ed. H. J. C. Grierson (Edinburgh: Scottish Academic Press, 1950), 125–26.

16. George Lukács, *The Historical Novel*, trans. Hannah and Stanley Mitchell (London: Merlin Press, 1962), 36.

17. *The Letters of Sir Walter Scott*, ed. H. J. C. Grierson (London: Constable, 1932), 1:342.

18. Croker, review of *Waverley*, 377.

19. Millgate, *Walter Scott*, 53.

20. David Daiches, "Scott's *Redgauntlet*," in *From Jane Austen to Joseph*

Conrad: Essays in Memory of James T. Hillhouse, ed. Robert C. Rothbun (Minneapolis: University of Minnesota Press, 1958), 54.

Chapter Five

1. Millgate, *Walter Scott*, 87.
2. Lockhart, *Memoirs*, 3:25–26.
3. Quoted in Andrew Lang, preface to *Guy Mannering*, Border Edition of the Waverley Novels (London: 1892–94).
4. Alexander Welsh, *The Hero of the Waverley Novels* (New Haven, Conn.: Yale University Press), 200.
5. Ibid., 212.
6. Review from *The British Ladies' Magazine*, quoted in *Scott: The Critical Heritage*, 104.
7. E. M. Forster, *Aspects of the Novel* ("rocks of cardboard," etc.) (New York: Harcourt, Brace, 1927), 53.

Chapter Six

1. Lockhart, *Memoirs*, 3:134.
2. Ibid., 3:131.
3. *Letters of Walter Scott*, 4:293.
4. Adolphus, *Letters*, 200.
5. Lockhart, *Memoirs*, 3:121.
6. Lukacs, *Historical Novel*, 36–37.
7. Review of *Tales of My Landlord*, in *Edinburgh Review*, March 1817, 216.

Chapter Seven

1. John Buchan, *Sir Walter Scott* (London: Cassell, 1932), 181.
2. Ibid., 183.
3. Leslie Fiedler, *Love and Death in the American Novel* (New York: Criterion Books, 1960), 167.
4. David Brown, *Walter Scott and the Historical Imagination* (London: Routledge & Kegan Paul, 1979), 111.
5. Quoted in *Scott: The Critical Heritage*, 111.
6. Ibid., 119.
7. Ibid., 120.
8. Ibid., 121.
9. Lockhart, *Memoirs*, 3:130.

Chapter Eight

1. Lockhart, *Memoirs*, 3:267.
2. Robin Mayhead, "*The Heart of Midlothian*: Scott as Artist," *Essays in Criticism*, July 1956, 266.

3. David Craig, *Scottish Literature and the Scottish People 1680–1830* (London: Chatto & Windus, 1961),   .
4. *Edinburgh Review*, March 1817, 196.

Chapter Nine

1. Edgar Johnson, *Sir Walter Scott: The Great Unknown*, 2 vols. (New York: Macmillan, 1970), 1:646.

Chapter Ten

1. Robert Cadell, Scott's publisher, quoted in Eric Quayle, *The Ruin of Sir Walter Scott* (London: Hart & Davis, 1968), 136.
2. Quoted in Johnson, *Sir Walter Scott: The Great Unknown*, 1:686.
3. Quoted in Alan Massie, "Scott and the European Novel," in *Sir Walter Scott: The Long-Forgotten Melody* ed. Alan Bold (London: Vision, 1983), 95.
4. Francis Hart, *Scott's Novels: The Plotting of Historical Survival* (Charlottesville: University of Virginia Press, 1966), 148.
5. Quoted in Edgar Rosenberg, *From Shylock to Svengali: Jewish Stereotypes in English Fiction* (Palo Alto, Calif.: Stanford University Press, 1960), 84.
6. William Hazlitt, *The Spirit of the Age* (Garden City, N.Y.: Doubleday, n.d.), 74.

Chapter Eleven

1. Samuel Coleridge, *Coleridge's Miscellaneous Criticism*, ed. T. M. Raysor (Cambridge, Mass.: Harvard University Press, 1940), 300.
2. Adolphus, *Letters*, 200.
3. Ibid., 201.
4. Ibid.
5. Review of *The Fortunes of Nigel*, *Quarterly Review*, July 1822, 339.
6. Reviews of *Tales of My Landlord*, *Quarterly Review*, January 1817, 432.
7. Lockhart, *Memoirs*, 3:417.
8. Lukács, *The Historical Novel*, 35.
9. Daiches, 86.
10. Judith Wilt, *Secret Leaves: The Novels of Sir Walter Scott* (Chicago: University of Chicago Press, 1985), 82.
11. Quoted in Craig, *Scottish Literature*, 250.
12. Review of *Tales of My Landlord*, *Edinburgh Review*, March 1817, 198.
13. Craig, *Scottish Literature*, 56.
14. Coleridge, *Coleridge's Miscellaneous Criticism*, 136.
15. Sidney Smith, quoted in Craig, *Scottish Literature*, 145.
16. Wood, 168 in Gordon, *Bicentennial Essays*.
17. Thomas Carlyle, "Sir Walter Scott," in *Criticism and Miscellaneous Essays* (New York: Scribners, 1896), 3:26.
18. *Journal*, 24 February 1828, 433.

19. Ibid.
20. *Quarterly Review*, July 1822, 339.
21. Daiches, 156.
22. Review of *The Fortunes of Nigel, Edinburgh Review*, March 1817, 223.
23. Quoted in Duncan Forbes, "The Rationalism of Sir Walter Scott," *Cambridge Quarterly*, October 1953, 26.
24. Coleridge, *Coleridge's Miscellaneous Criticism*, 341–42.
25. Fiedler, *Love and Death*, 167.
26. Cited in Lockhart, *Memoirs*, 3:22.
27. *Journal*, 13 October 664.
28. Ibid., 15 October 1831, 664.
29. Cited in Richard Stang, *The Theory of the Novel in England: 1850–1870* (New York: Columbia University Press, 1959), 202.
30. Coleridge, *Coleridge's Miscellaneous Criticism*, 322.
31. Wilt, *Secret Leaves*, 86.
32. Grierson, *Sir Walter Scott*, 68.
33. Quoted in Lockhart, *Memoirs*, 4:72.
34. Carlyle, "Sir Walter Scott," 83.
35. Sir Walter Scott, *The Works of John Dryden*, rev. George Saintsbury (Edinburgh: 1882), 1:663.
36. Coleridge, *Coleridge's Miscellaneous Criticism*, 335.
37. Adolphus, *Letters*, 41.
38. Fiedler, *Love and Death*, 154.
39. Grierson, *Sir Walter Scott*, 177.
40. Wilt, *Secret Leaves*, 42.
41. Robert Louis Stevenson, "A Gossip on Romance," in *Memories and Portraits* (New York: Charles Scribner & Sons, 1901), 264.
42. Henry James, *The Future of the Novel*, ed. Leon Edel (New York: Doubleday, 1956), 59.
43. Ibid., 60.
44. Forster, *Aspects*, 52.
45. R. F. Leavis, *The Great Tradition* (London: Chatto & Windus, 1948), 6.
46. Levine, *The Realistic Imagination*, 92.
47. Wilt, *Secret Leaves*, 17.
48. Walter Allen, *The English Novel: A Short Critical History* (London: Phoenix House, 1954), 53.
49. Massie, "Scott and the European Novel," 104.
50. Cited in Louis Maigron, *Le Roman historique a l'epoque romantique* (Paris: Honoré Champion, 1912), 52.
51. Massie, "Scott and the European Novel," 100.
52. Cited in Hillhouse, *The Waverley Novels*, 57.
53. Review of *Tales of My Landlord*, in *Edinburgh Review*, March 1817, 196.

Selected Bibliography

PRIMARY SOURCES

Poetry

The Complete Poetical Works of Sir Walter Scott. Edited by Horace E. Scudder. Boston: Houghton, Mifflin, 1898. A convenient and thoroughly annotated edition.
Minstrelsy of the Scottish Border. 2 vols. Kelso, Scotland: James Ballantyne, 1803.

The Waverley Novels (in chronological order)

Waverley, or 'Tis Sixty Years Since. Edinburgh: A. Constable, 1814.
Guy Mannering, or The Astrologer. Edinburgh: A. Constable, 1814.
The Antiquary. Edinburgh: A. Constable, 1816.
Tales of My Landlord. 1st ser. Edinburgh: William Blackwood, 1816. Includes *The Black Dwarf* and *Old Mortality.*
Tales of My Landlord. 2d ser. Edinburgh: A. Constable, 1818. *The Heart of Midlothian.*
Rob Roy. Edinburgh: A. Constable, 1818.
Tales of My Landlord. 3d ser. Edinburgh: A. Constable, 1819. Includes *The Bride of Lammermoor* and *A Legend of Montrose.*
Ivanhoe. Edinburgh: A. Constable, 1820.
The Monastery. Edinburgh: A. Constable, 1820.
The Abbot. Edinburgh: A. Constable, 1820.
Kenilworth. Edinburgh: A. Constable, 1821.
The Pirate. Edinburgh: A. Constable, 1822.
The Fortunes of Nigel. Edinburgh: A. Constable, 1822.
Peveril of the Peak. Edinburgh: A. Constable, 1822.
Quentin Durward. Edinburgh: A. Constable, 1823.
St. Ronan's Well. Edinburgh: A. Constable, 1823.
Redgauntlet: A Tale of the Eighteenth Century. Edinburgh: A. Constable, 1824.
Tales of the Crusaders. Edinburgh: A. Constable, 1825. Includes *The Betrothed* and *The Talisman.*
Woodstock, or The Cavalier. Edinburgh: A. Constable, 1826.
Chronicles of the Canongate: The Highland Widow, The Two Drovers, The Surgeon's Daughter. Edinburgh: Cadell, 1827.
Chronicles of the Canongate. 2d ser. Edinburgh: Cadell, 1829. Includes *St. Valentine's Day, or The Fair Maid of Perth.*

Anne of Geierstein, or The Maiden of the Mist. Edinburgh: Cadell, 1829.
Tales of My Landlord. 4th ser. London: Cadell, 1832. Includes *Count Robert of Paris* and *Castle Dangerous.*

Letters and Journals

The Journal of Sir Walter Scott, Edited by W. E. K. Anderson. London: Oxford University Press, 1972. Extensive annotation makes this edition almost a biography of Scott from 1826 to 1832.
The Letters of Sir Walter Scott, Edited by H. J. C. Grierson. 12 vols. London: Constable, 1932.
Scott on Himself: A Selection of the Autobiographical Writings of Sir Walter Scott. Edited by David Hewitt. Edinburgh: Scottish Academic Press, 1981.

Miscellaneous Prose

Letters on Demonology and Witchcraft. London: Cadell, 1830.
The Life of Napoleon Buonaparte, Emperor of the French. 9 vols. London: Cadell, 1827.
Lives of the Novelists. London: Oxford University Press, 1906. Originally published as introductions to individual volumes of the Novelist's Library (London, 1821–25).
Miscellaneous Works of Sir Walter Scott. Edited by John Gibson Lockhart, 28 vols. Edinburgh: Cadell, 1834–36. Most nearly complete collection of Scott's nonfictional prose.
The Prefaces to the Waverly Novels. Edited by Mark A. Weinstein. Lincoln: University of Nebraska Press, 1978.
The Works of John Dryden, With Notes and a Life of the Author. 18 vols. London, 1808.
The Works of Jonathan Swift. . . . With Notes and a Life of the Author. 19 vols. London, 1814.

SECONDARY SOURCES

Books

Adolphus, John Leycester. *Letters to Richard Heber, Esq. Containing Critical Remarks on the Series of Novels Beginning with "Waverley" and an Attempt to Ascertain Their Author.* London: Rodell & Martin, 1822. First extended piece of Scott criticism; discusses characteristics common to the poems and the novels.
Alexander, J. H., editor. *Scott and His Influence.* Aberdeen: Association for Scottish Literary Studies, 1983.
Ball, Margaret. *Sir Walter Scott as a Critic of Literature.* New York: Columbia University Press, 1907. A convenient summary of Scott's critical opinions.

Bradley, Philip. *An Index to the Waverley Novels.* Metuchen, N.J.: Scarecrow Press, 1975. This book attempts "to locate persons, things, places, words, phrases, proverbs, etc., to arrange a number of persons by trade or profession, and of things by subject."

Buchan, John. *Sir Walter Scott.* London: Cassell, 1932. A highly readable and sympathetic biography, including much criticism.

Corson, J. C. A. *A Bibliography of Scott: A Classified and Annotated List of Books and Articles Relating to His Life and Works, 1797–1940.* Edinburgh: Oliver & Boyd, 1943.

Dekker, George. "An American Scott: Imitation of Exploration and Criticism." In *James Fenimore Cooper the Novelist.* London: Routledge & Kegan Paul, 1967, 20–42. Sees Scott's influence on Cooper's work as decisive. Deals principally with Cooper's first two novels, *The Spy* and *Lionel Lincoln.*

Frye, Northrop. *The Secular Scripture: A Study of the Structure of Romance.* Cambridge, Mass.: Harvard University Press, 1976. Makes reference to use and parody of traditional romance elements in the Waverley Novels: the lost identity of the heir, the mirror image or twins, the descent into an outlawed society, and the animal or inarticulate human companion.

Grierson, H. J. C. *Sir Walter Scott, Bart: A New Life Supplementary to, and Corrective of, Lockhart's Biography.* London: Constable, 1938. Concerned primarily with Scott's business affairs, but includes valuable critical comments.

Hart, Francis R. *Scott's Novels: The Plotting of Historical Survival.* Charlottesville: University of Virginia Press, 1966. A generally admiring survey, emphasizing the diversity of the novels.

Hayden, John O., editor. *Scott: the Critical Heritage.* New York: Barnes & Noble, 1970. Reprints contemporary reviews of the novels and poems, Victorian critical essays, and brief comments by Goethe, Heine, Stendhal, Balzac, Mark Twain, and others; stops at 1883.

Hillhouse, James T. *The Waverley Novels and Their Critics.* Minneapolis: University of Minnesota Press, 1936. Valuable summary of critical opinion from 1814 to the time of publication.

Jeffares, A. Norman, editor. *Scott's Mind and Art.* Edinburgh: Oliver & Boyd, 1969. A substantial and wide-ranging collection of general essays dealing with the novels, principally the 1940s through 1960s.

Johnson, Edgar. *Sir Walter Scott: The Great Unknown.* 2 vols. New York: Macmillan, 1970. Detailed and highly sympathetic; includes commentary on each novel. Replaces Lockhart as the standard biography.

Lockhart, John Gibson. *Memoirs of the Life of Sir Walter Scott.* 5 vols. New York: Houghton Mifflin, 1902. A compilation rather than a biography, including much material from Scott's letters and journals and long quotations from contemporary reviews. Facts are sometimes altered, even invented, to brighten the portrait of Scott.

McMaster, Graham. *Scott and Society.* Cambridge: Cambridge University Press,

1981. Detailed study of Scott's opinions on politics and the nature of society, and their intellectual origins.

Millgate, Jane. *Walter Scott: The Making of the Novelist.* Toronto: University of Toronto Press, 1984. Concentrates on the first half-dozen novels, taking them as an ongoing series. Concerned with the creation of the author of the Waverley Novels as a literary persona and the Waverley Novels as an entity.

Quayle, Eric. *The Ruin of Sir Walter Scott.* London: Hart & Davis, 1967. Attacks the sentimental myth of Scott's goodness and greatness created by Lockhart; asserts that Scott's "status-seeking land hunger" caused his ruin. A useful corrective to both Lockhart's and Johnson's biographies.

Rubenstein, Jill. *Sir Walter Scott: A Reference Guide.* Boston: G. K. Hall & Co., 1978. Annotated bibliography of writings about Scott, 1932–77.

Shaw, Harry E. *The Forms of Historical Fiction: Sir Walter Scott and His Successors.* Ithaca, N.Y.: Cornell University Press, 1983. Deals especially with the ideology of the novels, the treatment of the hero, and his relationship to society.

Tulloch, Graham. *The Language of Walter Scott: A Study of His Scottish and Period Language.* London: Deutsch, 1980. An extremely detailed study of the Scots language in itself and as it is used in the Waverley Novels. Also studies Scott's use of "period" vocabulary and grammatical forms.

Welsh, Alexander. *The Hero of the Waverley Novels.* New Haven: Yale University Press, 1963. A thoughtful and stimulating discussion of the "passive hero," the "dark hero," and the motifs of honor, property, and anxiety in the novels. An essential book.

Wilt, Judith. *Secret Leaves: The Novels of Sir Walter Scott.* Chicago: University of Chicago Press, 1985. Sees Scott's great subject as the transition from a protobourgeois world of romance and of oral culture to the nineteenth-century world of realism, rationality, and textuality.

Articles and Sections of Books

Anderson, James. "Sir Walter Scott as Historical Novelist: Scott's Opinions on Historical Fiction." *Studies in Scottish Literature* 4 (July 1966):29–41; (October 1966): 63–78; (January 1967):155–78; 5 (July 1967):14–27; (October 1967):83–97; (January 1968):143–66. A thorough analysis, including Scott's general attitude toward the past, his treatment of nationality, his handling of literary and historical sources, his choice of historical figures, and his use of language, among other topics.

Bagehot, Walter. "The Waverley Novels." In *Literary Studies.* Vol. 2. London: Longmans, Green, 1879. Reprinted in *Scott: The Critical Heritage,* edited by John Hayden (see above). Representative Victorian opinion; praises Scott's moral "soundness" but deprecates the superficiality of his characterizations.

Carlyle, Thomas. "Sir Walter Scott." In *Critical and Miscellaneous Essays,* 3:22–88. New York: Scribner's, 1896.

Coleridge, Samuel. *Coleridge's Miscellaneous Criticism.* Edited by T. M. Raysor.

Cambridge, Mass.: Harvard University Press, 1940. Coleridge's scattered remarks include the most penetrating contemporary criticism of Scott's poems and novels, and anticipate much twentieth-century criticism.

Craig, David. *Scottish Literature and the Scottish People, 1680–1830.* London: Chatto & Windus, 1961. Includes a highly informative and suggestive discussion of the social and linguistic situation in which Scottish writers of the early nineteenth century found themselves.

Daiches, David. "Scott's Achievement as a Novelist." *Nineteenth Century Fiction* 6 (September 1951):80–95; (December 1951):153–73. The best of the Waverley Novels derive their tension from the author's ambivalence toward historical "progress," with its accompanying loss of tradition and possibilities for heroic action.

————. "Scott's *Redgauntlet.*" In *From Jane Austen to Joseph Conrad: Essays in Memory of James T. Hillhouse,* edited by Robert C. Rathbun. Minneapolis: University of Minnesota Press, 1958. Interprets *Redgauntlet* as Scott's *Don Quixote.*

Fiedler, Leslie. *Love and Death in the American Novel.* New York: Criterion Books, 1960. Many suggestive comments on the thematic significance of Scott's novels and their influence on American fiction.

Forster, E. M. *Aspects of the Novel.* New York: Harcourt, Brace, 1927. Devastating attack on style, construction, and characterization in the Waverley Novels.

Garside, Philip. "Scott and the 'Philosophical' Historians." *Journal of the History of Ideas* 36 (July 1975):497–512. Studies effect of the "philosophical" historians of the eighteenth century and their concern with the history of social institutions on Scott's concept of history and on the Waverley Novels.

Gordon, S. Stewart. "*Waverley* and the 'Unified Design.'" *English Literary History* 18 (June 1951):107–22. Argues the unity of Waverley; action springs from the central character, and scenery, events, and other characters all reveal or influence the development of the central figure.

Hazlitt, William. "Why Heroes of Romance Are Insipid." In *Complete Works of William Hazlitt.* Vol. 17. Edited by P. P. Howe. London: J. M. Dent & Sons, 1933. Originally published in *New Monthly Magazine* (November 1827). A contemporary apology for the passive hero of the Waverley Novels.

Kettle, Arnold. *Introduction to the English Novel.* 2 vols. London: Hutchinson University Library, 1953. Chapter 3, "Scott: *The Heart of Midlothian,*" praises this novel for its broad societal range and presentation of social tensions but finds a loss of power when Scott requires Jeanie Deans, the peasant girl, to surrender her freedom of action to the paternalistic Duke of Argyll.

Levine, George. *The Realistic Imagination: English Fiction from Frankenstein to Lady Chatterley.* Chicago: University of Chicago Press, 1981. Chapters 3 and 4, dealing with *Waverley, The Bride of Lammermoor,* and *Redgauntlet,* present Scott as an essential figure in the development of literary realism in the English novel.

Lukács, George. *The Historical Novel.* Translated by Hannah Mitchell and Stanley Mitchell. London: Merlin Press, 1962. Surprisingly sympathetic Marxist criticism, concerned primarily with Scott's treatment and philosophy of history.

Morgan, Susan. "Old Heroes and a New Heroine in the Waverley Novels." *English Literary History* 50 (Fall 1983):559–87. Sees the Waverley Novels as defining humane values, affirmed by the official heroes, and most fully expressed by Jeanie Deans in *The Heart of Midlothian*, in contrast to "masculine" concepts of heroism exemplified by the doomed "dark heroes."

Rosenberg, Edgar. *From Shylock to Svengali.* Palo Alto, Calif.: Stanford University Press, 1960. Chapter 4, "The Jew as Clown and the Jew's Daughter," studies Scott's use and development of Jewish stereotypes in *Ivanhoe*, but also sees Isaac and Rebecca as embodying the novel's basic themes of estrangement and dispossession.

Stevenson, Robert Louis. "A Gossip on Romance," *Memories and Portraits.* New York: Charles Scribner & Sons, 1901. Sees Scott as a "dreamer" rather than an artist.

Woolf, Virginia. "Sir Walter Scott." In *The Moment.* New York: Harcourt, Brace, 1948. Defense of Scott against his modern detractors by a leading modernist.

Index